W9-DAM-357

chasing

the

bluebird

Val Villarreal, Jr.

 FriesenPress

Suite 300 - 990 Fort St
Victoria, BC, V8V 3K2
Canada

www.friesenpress.com

N. V. Krogius' book, Chess Pscychology, quoted in the back of the book entry.

ISBN
978-1-5255-3086-9 (Hardcover)
978-1-5255-3087-6 (Paperback)
978-1-5255-3088-3 (eBook)

1. POETRY

Distributed to the trade by The Ingram Book Company

PREFACE

Just filling in the blanks.
Enjoy!

"... what if

eternity is a line

trillions of light-years long, and

time

    is a pencil dot

on that line?

The interesting thing is not

that this dot is <u>on</u> that line, but that ...

it is part <u>of</u>

    that line."

VVJ

A CLOSING FIELD

The ground is cut and ready for use,
but nothing's set to grow,
lest memories stand and wait beyond the meadow's low;
the neighbors think in crests, as if in thought
beyond some nadir's peak, this side
of a holding-water spout no human ever knows.

Could be the rains empty
in their cry for long-lost land; could be
the crying empties for our own betterment
        amid mankind's vacant sea.
And it might be found that memories last longer
than the door that opens
onto a field called "you and me".

A GAMUT OF TALES...

The house is warm;
the coffee brews well here,
but no one turns from your eye
to tell you "No."
Sweaters are worn
　　　　　　　(but no one sees the trees
for the forest's rustic feel) ...
　　　The coffee is warm,
and the house brews well
　　　　　　　(a gamut of tales).

ACCEPTING THE UNFINISHED

The aura of the times,
the multi-faceted look there given,
lies taut against the backdrop
of an all-will-be-well-if-we-leave-well-enough-alone thing.
The past is always at arm's length, ready for viewing,
but only as a problem—
may we savor parts of it, forget the rest,
and let loose the lesser dogs of war.

SELF-HAVENED PEOPLE

And what hurt may a delusional program do?
One mishap here or there may just erase itself in the long
run ...
but what if it doesn't?
Can we afford such a gaffe?
Self-havened people—
a people who will to accept the unfinished
                as finished!

A CHERISHED GLORY

A plant is a cherished thing—
a growing entity onto her own, one which seeks

the light simply, and yet, unlike ourselves,
never moves to obtain that glory—never bothers...

though the quiet of an evening lasts fully
(or so we perceive).

These sirens live eternally;
their patience

in the light of day allows them to sail
                              past the moon's shine

on an eternal frame of mind.

A GOOD STOPPED

The falling away
of a product,
which stuns the public
into non-reliance
and dissolution,
polarizes elements.
Constants long-ago won
are now razed, holds barred,
lay non-administered.
The good fostered
by its ouster runs dry;
the water lines,
after years of ease,
cake and fail
   in legalese.

—A HOUSE DIVIDED

The snowy form of fog dabbles in insincerity

and verifies in false humor; it indoctrinates the air with fool's
gold ideas

to the point that it is left holding a non-congenial pan,

unreflective of the suppleness and beauty of the forthcom-
ing day.

Its fall is tender, without transparency, with wishes to
be softer

than the white presumed.

Woe!

"Such is the state of things in the world today." So sings the
song of our fathers,

now torn to bits, tooled on an anvil that scorches the eye:
the "knowing"

of our fellow men. This present snow hovers over those lids

and scoffs at the knowledge long-ago learned, long-
ago accepted,

long-ago resolved:

If a house divided stands,

who is it that stands?

—A LATTER DAY IN JANUARY

A latter day in January,
wedged between a juncture and its walls
like an alley cat caught
        and too-long weary.
The winter's edge is parsed—
      wild and rude.
Exuberance tires, streams stall,
dancers to the tune of a solstice's ruse.

Other days are warm, lie crudely shaped
in their early drop of
summer; sheltered man lives in this sweeter jam
of heat—
                that sugar-tilting drummer.

But the little child subsists in this winter's woe,
a landed seed two-stepped
      along the way.

—A MALEFICENT SHOW!

What is the malice of being alive

and not knowing whether the ends ever flow

through the gaps in the torment of a decision's results?

If all that we know

branches into our system,

and then rails to the skies like the honeyed thought's
arrogant hive,

how can the ends not irreparably grow

into maleficent show?

—A MASTERPIECE!

...and the sea keeps swirling
like a never-ending song longing for forgiveness
and a heart to sympathize; Oh, the cruelness
of waves—
        but what a masterpiece: a life
on a constant mend,
                and no stops!
Spinning,
    spinning...
and churning without end.

—A MOTHER'S CRY

It's interesting how an individual can be viewed
as if without an apparent essence or without a modicum
of being;
the person's movement towards you commences, is cued,
but your evidence is slim, it strains unseeing.

The individual's heart is in the right place, attended to
with the surest of humility and a want and need
for compassion,
but however much your code and ethic bends—however new
your past views—its panoply is an old invention.

Words are voiced with the feel of holiday mind;
even the seizure in the vowels wrests from the air a love
for humankind.
And the other's look is distant—in a bind—
the door quietly closing on this parting, bluntly signed.

AND SHE GROWS

The horizontals are obvious to the viewer;
so too are the verticals, curving as they do in latitudes.

The patterned cage is wild enough, encompassing as it does
a weightless cover: ourselves.

No windows there, but openings—
in and of themselves not openings, but barred screams,

unscreened and long evolved; man, a careened side,
a ball, a feather…

The young girl sees with the eyes of an even younger age,
but what she knows she evaluates beyond her.

Notes are passed, father to daughter, in pings,
in ditto language, and she grows,

and the father caroms off its sides
like a ball, light as a feather, and just as seeing.

—A HIDDEN THING

This will be a hidden thing.

It will encase itself, yet race through corridors nimbly;

sighing at times, it will reform differently.

It will slowly make itself known, forming my center's core.

It will lend me tools, for progress fits
                            like hand and glove.

And I will one day genuflect in kindness as co-distributer
        and say:

"I have always sensed you, stayed near you."

[For humility resonates in positive humor; though hidden,
        it evokes completeness.]

ARRIVING

The walk is a long one,
leading up to the ease with which we live,
dangling before us like a spider's web,
long-lived, wispy, and solid,
but with the aura of distance and sharp separation;
birth is difficult, yet a matter of truth:
      child to gut!
Feel your way through the copula's form and round it,
      specifically;
once there, we can say (with a mother's voice),
"We have arrived."

—A SHORT QUIP

The limits to life are many—

so too is completeness ushering through—

however much one wills to chase it, to revitalize its
inner ties,

so too falls

the whimsical cut in the cropped bush,

this blossoming flower, this thing which pulls us
toward effrontery

and dangles

like a sword to resistance.

Our sentence is verified; the article's humor

done.

—A TIME LIVED

A time lived,
framed for our lot,
self-willed,
postponed by the ungodly,
    love-short.
We are its drive,
and we are its satisfactory feel.

A time lived,
always journeying,
the yelps of the hound…
who can say
what is uneven sand,
the good
and the bad
with the lay of the land?

— PAIN

Pain is on a holiday,
and all thought is gone,
but he telegraphs, in dots,
    the griever's song.

His journey's return is stepped up;
his will
is for circumstances,
        and his heart is still.

I see this face—inhuman,
out of the ordinary,
a trip into harshness, an easy clip—
pain is on a holiday,
and all thought is gone,
he telegraphs, in dots,
    the griever's song.

I pry no more;
I simply acquiesce, stellar-less,
down the hallway
to the dry and waterless.
(His journey's return is stepped up;
his will
is for circumstances,
and his heart is still.)

—AT THE MASTER'S SEAT

A matter told swings ahead;

trends run cold abridged in lead—

contiguous chance and good intention

are never danced without invention.

Into this way, our heads' will stalemated,

we brew, step-rated.

Among the many, some will to be complete—

though only at table replete.

—THE WORLD, STILL!

Off steeples words abound,
flaring down curves like breasts on a gargoyle;
they are avidly throated, deafening bells swinging tenuously
from palpitating eaves—

so much for our song's reticence.

What in most hearts can't be found is being said today!

Waterspouts lure the all from most of us;
barkers and snake-oil swindlers swivel over our heads,
with each their wire and coil.

They roll through the ages at cost,
tied as we are to their torment, and of our own fear cooled...

The song will not end,
for its fame falls not from its height;
in this roiling fervor, we shadow in anger
from truth and beneficent light,
held in a bind ... a world of bombardment
from
the world, still.

—THE NEED TO FILL SPACE!

The need to fill space!

...our paper's edges do nothing for us, nor do the lines
themselves...

The sphere, which hears our words,
dances to that music only we could have composed; it
streams like the color black

across a flat plane, seeking to tell a lie
or two...

Yet, here sits a type of beauty few can take away,

few can reach,
sack;

this beauty lies

in the sentence taken,

in its stops,

in how it runs—

(There are no qualifying limits
to beauty.)

—THE LIST

"... bread,
no below-the-ground matter,
no substances borrowed,
no basting lost,
surety of performance bought,
more bread,

object:
to keep the fire burning
and stay warm ..."

She loosened her bracelet and walked down
the aisle.

BRING ON MY RETURN,
AND I WILL RETURN!

Bring on my return and I will return!

Take hold of the brine, if you can; let it slip through
your fingers,

and tell all your mates to have done with the past.

Let them trail through their shackles as freemen and
true voyagers;

the return is at hand.

> The winds have been altered
> towards advancement.

Return, I say, and be formed amid the lowering sky,

See!

The rush of the past has been quelled by my peace,

and the avalanching ways of man have unraveled and been
made plain.

Everything—take everything you revolve upon and toss it
into the sea;

all you have held to breast, pour overboard—the vaulted sails
bring down.

Bring on my return and I will return!

[from Jeremiah, 31:18]

BRUISING QUIETLY

The luxurious taste for the food at hand

reflects non-insatiably on the shining implicitness

of the plate on which it sits:

a massive and corrosive advance to be one with the comfort

of foundation.

Our eyes need not quest for the better frame

in the settling of the matter mid the tag, which it settles
and gives;

it need only rest in sigh

and bruise quietly.

—EASY PICKINGS

Easy pickings
trailing from torn edges
parked close to ground
like seeds rolled—
       stems,
but only to the mind's eye.
No one need see the thing evolve,
for that interest
is anything
but a waiting search for stance—
the future end-state.

EDGES

Edges titter in the bounce or fall,

like an oblong thought on a moth-eaten shawl

that caters to an atmospheric blue, stopped by a
rolling skew

and a wobbling rake to its weighty chew.

Of the burdens carried there's little to do; the
pause long-ago
                          made—

the turning in the journey totteringly laid,

long-ago new.

—NO CAPTIONS NEEDED

The state of non-achievement clasps
in the quiet of pretension,
to the social ease stamped on the head of everyman,
like a battle won through no effort.
This scent of rights stands at attention in fettered fatigue
onto the facades
of worn-out buildings and burning flesh!
Could this be tied to centered non-connectedness—
to that which usurps and entrenches?
We ride roughshod and loose,
deep into the forests of a free and predicated patriotism
                              feigned.
[No captions needed.]
.

—IT NEVER DIES

The rose is colored yellow
on the frame
against a dirt-pink brick and ash-filled wood—
this vision forms from above.
I touch the feathered bud.
(It never dies
    or grows,
    and lights the sky-like wall.)

ITS DOOR TO DESIRE

I sense time.

Its many colors freeze,
unduly torn
      from its secured installment;

the cold insures warmth,
but its memory shadows,

and its door

[to desire]

      veers,

    and   postpones.

FAR FROM KISS

The soft green leaves,

tattering in the wind and aged at the tips, rust

on an extra-bounded effigy—

sky-grown as they are.

.

And what remains?

      The task at hand:

To grow by seed,

      far from kiss.

—FILLERS

There are fillers within to tell us when our words are right;
they warn us of the sun's intensity,

of its light and wonder, its ponder on a distant sea!
The bracelets ringing in the background,

the child's engaging sound, even the movement of a scrap-
ing chair
in the turn around

touches the ear like sparks from the blue,
and in earnest we sense this ratio: dew to grass;

and what must pass
(once these voices rise beyond themselves

above the garments and the shelves)
is a quiet outer issue walling all surroundings.

These shakes
and these transitional moves

re-stage the setting and all the passing grooves—
revitalized ownership from within.

(To shun this must be sin.)

FIRST TO LAST

We were the first to reach the golden ring,
the first to think in time,
and the first to say almost anything just to see it rhyme.

We were the first to touch the golden skies
as children on a swing,
and words were said to the wise: Rise as one to sing.

But love requires
we be honest squires,
that we hold these means to the ends;
it requires that gifts
never ground those fires
  which God to others gives.

We were the first to teach a lesser world,
the first to feed the few—
and it's sad to say that nothing's old if nothing's ever
right or new.

We were the first to claim the better way,
to say its time had come,
but to think as first there must first stray the fear-
less some.

And love requires
we be honest squires,
that we hold these means to the ends;

it requires that gifts
never ground those fires
    which God to others gives.

—GOING SHIRTLESS

The hurt is moot—
no danger rises but to sentence me to the tomb!

My personal references shall claim my being,
and stillness stands beside me; it succumbs.

I brace for its promulgations.
I brew in an easy keg of finely broiled hops,

and what I see may not surprise me;
non-dual assurance

     embraces all contingent paths—
it would be a matter of limiting myself to the facts, were it not
truer to say

the facts have me.
         They roll unchained about me like a label's rub.

—GOOGLING!

How to find the perfect shop,
How to take a test,
How to dream in lemonade,
How to stop and rest,
How to pass the other guy,
How to steal a peach,
How to raise a cup of tea,
How to never teach,
How to stay forever blind,
How to make a fist…
(How to stop the manufactured prop
and end a bliss of lists!)

—GROUNDHOG DAY

It's not a matter of bravery—
of stepping up to the plate and wryly saying, "Yes!

A three-tiered homer!"
Of falling on your face, and getting up, opting to
fall again

just to prove the fall was real.
The morning rise is always a struggle;

in the first place, one must open one's eyes,
seek a line of sight, blink,

and keep to resistance—
the clinker, the hair in the soup?

Where the hell and what on this earth am I?
Is this the remedy

or just another empty promise?
Finally, you close your eyes, hit the snooze,

and forget this rising ever happened.
The next thing you know, it's February.

One would think that upon seeing one's own shadow
one would also see!

HAIL TO THE FIRE

The heat is not yet here,
and the circumstances erupting from the dye
in the quiet stale of the weaning sky
are far from dear;
there are no tales to tell of grasses
lining the savannas, or wild beasts approaching
the camps,
no free-wheeled bathing to be found by the seas
on the sloping French ramps.

Only time is at hand,
and onto this ground step the possibilities
rolling like fronts diminishing, and...
from these sensibilities,
stand I before this heretical crest,
trolling like a demon sensually done, but hail
to the fire, dropped under me abreast
the immortality beyond this mortal rail!
May such a quest fail.

—HARBORING ALIBIS

She promenades through her passion, sets it afire,

stretches herself helplessly over it, inflamed as she is

for the budding pinnacle of her desire.

None but the air she breathes hampers her, none, in the
whole of her armory,

        veers to stall this illusion—to alleviate
its long-pressing intrusion.

        Every move gears itself up for the opportuni-
        ties availed;

all dance before her like dithyrambs from the failing past,
          targeted as she is

by this whim in her mind.

        In the quiet, her rooms
        lie sinister,

vying for space among this desolately-riveted claim;
         the faces in her dogma

sadly pale amid the shadowy forms now looming.

And the question arises:

What will she do,

in this state wherein nothing may be traded for and
nothing given?

She stills her heart per this dilemma

(as for an edict striven).

—HARPING

Swerving toward a line
when that line fails to move, steering
onto it, independently of view, or willfulness
seems to me to be off its intended end;
not knowing we do this is tantamount
to an idea's winsome window tour.
The line was meant to be,
in the eyes of astute sympathy—an assured place
for measuring rectitude, for enhancing the
right weave
through paths stumbled upon.
But why harp on the negative
when the positive nature of things changes
  with change itself?

—HONORING THE GAME

Honoring the game
is like placing your trust on a set system
and going with it; the valor
in the rhyme and easy pull of the run and stance
found surges through the mind
like an adrenaline-filled piece of chocolate.
But games end, and in their place
forms a vacuum, much like the air in a balloon extracted
and visually tossed on a table; it vilifies
the trust one has entered in.
So, you continue with your own methods, extending
the ridden horse unto death and beyond.
You take the mantle and add a stitch;
you clarify the end and accentuate the ruling stop.
One move endorses the whim; another ensures
all the vigor that was found in the game itself. Only
a truth is interwoven into it as if to finalize
the whole before your eyes.
The game is still sitting,
            but on another's pedestal-rivets.

—HOW STRANGE

No man's land, where our walks mind the fallen

and the fog broils over stagnancy for the strange

that stare in the odd man's weave.

We harbor in expectancy—

in a sea of instant response and quick stops,

on the strange: the monster we fight.

(If we only knew how strange we all are…

                          how strange, how strange…)

—IN A QUANDARY, OCEANS DEEP!

How differently must I think before I'm ousted by
my comrades?

How differently must I proceed?

To lose my life?

To lose my property, how must I walk, or talk?

How must I be received to be sanctioned for loss?

Can my rights run loose and useless?

And indeed, may I call myself society's pariah?

Shall I never wear their firm esteem?

How should I endure mankind's scorn,

impure being, innocent, yet unbelieved and abandoned?

"Lest they should be shunned in their turn."

—Go in peace you say;

Master of my domain, omnipotent all,

Creator of lowest and highest, and still less loved.

How should I proceed?

From the depths I praise you; behold this outer shell.

Where is your everlasting equanimity?

Where this unresolved love?

I breathe,

but I fail to sense.

—IN LENORE-SLEEP

The darkness, which folds
into madness and falling night,
reaches from the marching heels of holds
in our inner-light.
It might be saved from the glue,
which seeks to take us through the mill—
this past we never knew
or mnemonic thought at work post-work still!

For when this depth is touched on,
and through the day beyond us lingers,
we tend like Doe-lost John
to trod afoul the handle's wringers.
Now laden to the cubical of war,
we toss in journey, into growing shrinkage
like a star
united to its linkage.

(Deep into the wake
of quick forgetfulness, a Lenore-
    like sleep rolls
       across life's scrimmage.)

—IN OUR IMMINENT DENIAL!

Where might we dance in the halls of our own quiet glance
to the fixtures now laid,
feast on the tables where the best of the least trace and
gambol in far-fetched thoughts,
in their ramble caught quick (like a flatly-broken walking
stick) on a path
sun-ridden, with good imbued,
                    but irreverently rude?
On which ground may we form on firmness untold, noting
the short-lived avenues
which languish in curvature not sanctioned
by society's needs (and its forthcoming anxiously-
linked combustibility)?
And will the event reform for our sake, drench us
with clues—with the answers forewarned of in that enjoy-
able book?
I sense we here now live on this isle,
and that the pounding of the keys even more will resound in
our imminent denial!

—IN THE BEATING OF HEART

In the beating of heart lies the touch that radiates

in the mind of the lover; he wounds without wounding—

how beautifully field the heavens here...

how brutally free.

—IN THE PELTED GRAY OF MIND

Breaking down the scaffolding—

it would have been

spectacular had not the fly in the oint-
ment scenario

intruded,

found the evidence wanting,

filled as it was with a non-talk kind of pelting.

There can be no holding on to the
sandy porousness

of rude encumbrance.

IT'S A SMALL SEA!

It's a small sea,
this world and its vastness.

It harbors the whole of the universe
in the sharpest of form.

Nothing dulls it nor cuts it quickly
but that it will heal eternally,

and your greeting,
within its proximate boundaries, sits good

to the coming end,
it's placed in the heavens

as if in the depths of a well—
Oh, to be there!

—LET US SEE

We might demurely hold for tomorrow and be quick
     and insecure;

to demur would be worse
      (we might sail past today too unsure).

Let us see what the times bring,
      but note its humorous offering;

we may yet find the proof-ridden course
      on its back quietly suffering!

—LIFE'S MATTER

Life's matter?

To be free of sect,

encasement …

to shun "correct".

This policy's overview?

A quiet not found among those

who over-do,

for death is a rose,

its life so true.

—LIKE THE SAILOR TIED

It's always quiet after a storm;

only the wind cherishes, in voluptuous pull,

the stirring silence of the morning's darker hue;

it crawls past issues not yet ripe, dull

to the riveting heat of yesterday's padded news; over

and under this wresting insurgency climbs

those riveting arms, carrying her pining lover no more.

And yet,

there will come a time when the energies extended

over dimming synergy

must reign free of selfish insistence, ending

in fronted effigy.

There will come a time when these wanton needs fall fast

in the abandonment of hope.

There will come a time. There will come a time,

and it will last—

like the sailor tied to his mast.

—LONG-LIVED AND SETTLED

A tainted letter never says anything;
it merely spots the ink, re-administers it to a two-
point conversion,
wraps it away nicely in a wad of reflective white, crumpled...
The statement only satisfies the fact it has been issued,
its lettering dismantled onto a myriad
of off-shoot molecules no dark matter could hold even with
its eyes open.
Whose ink was it? From which office did it evolve? And why
was the sending imminent to these times?
This day is a blotted day, to some an important addition to
the Weltanschauung persisting in the heart of this world's
purview—a coagulating movement
drying in the open sun waiting for the fly in the juice to form.
It is history, but not of the collectible kind—not of
the savoring-of-the-memory
                                    kind.
Simply told, it is the worn residue from a board long-lived
and settled,
long-lived and settled.

MEASURED FLOODING

It's funny how a flood measures the times.

Untroubled waters are
but the tabled ramifications of things unruled,
strictly functional...

Wires, which long to be black too long,
spark ... hanging potentially.
The freedom founded on such a gimmick plunges
beneath the deeper well of true understanding.

The errors are many, the issues brewing
thereof plentiful,
but the honey refuses to come.

I'm guessing that the essence of the eve-
ning's foolishness
fails in the feverish effervescent fortitude
    to some given.

—ON MEETING LIGHT

A different order gathers
whole and complete and externally native.
Further off, an eddy bolsters endlessly…
It vilifies this fruit, for its alien nature is ruth-
lessly imported,
encased as it is in its pull.
It unravels and loosens it,
but only to have it unwind even more unrelatedly
and strange—
an unknown light qualified exotically
                              to an unknown sphere.

I sit and listen
and praise this thing un-wistfully—
there, I've said it,
and I thereby reveal myself.

—MOLDED

The drought is faulted for not being fair, for trouncing

the pastures and leaving them bare;

and the many hoofed marks, the myriad meanings tiered
forwardly, end.

This is understood, as lightening is understood, as the docility
of these times

is understood and gingerly liquidated. This ravishing pelt

ceases to care for the ground; it renounces aim, stops only ...
to visualize torment.

My heart palpitates like a bird in its dumb thought,

                    and human urgency takes a
                    back seat!

The extra step never arrives;

into disarray and decay positives move

molded

                    and stunted by unhappy groove.

MOVING WITH THE FLOW

Could be that islands are simply rocks moving with the flow
of the few that need not grow.

Light shines briskly onto their silver backing—a beam
shining from a border too far away.

This seeing is given to man by man
for the ordering of heart,

and eyes sharply dot along the sea's edge to see
what they may not:

an understanding parsed by ligament and wool
and similarly blanched to fit an empty sky.

I notice that an angel sits on the starry night's darkness.

(It could very well be that islands are simply rocks moving
with the flow
of the few that need not grow.)

—MY DEAREST STONE

I have often thought of you in the quiet rustle of
the marketplace,

in the easy hassle of the conveniences you form. I trace,

in the cramped elusiveness of emptying space, your first
attempts at belonging.

Compromises come to mind, the giving up

on circumstances arriving, ending

in a vorticity of blend from which all suggestions turn

and drop and rend,

given the reticence found, the fall in the continually rising
cosmos eternally juggling

like a coin on an enveloped send; there is no sense

to the insurmountable woe

now entering time; so,

if thought of you must stand, like a bas-relief show, then—

let it be so:

Stand my dearest stone as a once-long-
ago known.

—MY UNDERSTANDING'S METER

There is nothing racing towards me closer than the sea;
nothing searches for me like this shore's bristling sands,
aching to be one
with the revivifying water's edges springing into view. As
I nurture
on this understated understanding, I bend in certainty to its
newness. It toughens me
and sanctifies me; it reinvents me, nourishes me—
it heralds the dawn of a wounded mind on an easy breeze.
This line is coastal, churched before me; its apse salted by the
weight of sky
            laden in rock.
This does not alarm me, nor does its quelling rush of
fevered substance
dissemble the heart. None dares say, "I have been there."
None dares say, "This is pure heaven." None dares say, "Follow
me and rise."
This stays eternally, crawls proximally. This revelation
            moves in an always-event, tooled well.
This is my understanding's rhyme, and my understand-
ing's meter,
           and my poem's long-affecting industry.
           And I welcome it.

NERVES AS MESSENGERS

Nerves are the messengers

in a system that seeks to right a wrong

as we muster along in this half-baked world we
ive in;

they trip us up when faltering,

revitalize us when the need avails itself...

Their awkward nature

is seen most exquisitely

when our will to forge ahead is less than
stellar (and

short on whim).

—NEWNESS

The push is of a pen long lost to mankind.

It brings back memories, delineates itself from the run of
the mill

matter-of-fact push... It works backward from the history of
things like a clock

tuned

to the makeshift ticking of a heart

long-ago dead, yet still hungering for the continuity resolved

by its then-streaming avenue;

and the things penned then pose powerful to the mind.

Change must poignantly burst open.

Its new dot not just hovering like a thought in a past sky
but waxed—

upon paper waxed—pressed by this beginning long ended;

it is a pen still at work

[but with a newness in the bargain].

NO FIND!

Walking,
chewing gum,
generating,
culling, atmospheric—
air,
nerves,
stillness,
tentativeness,
pursuer's arms
[Dionysian]—
no respite,
interfering posture,
a staring down,
no repair,
requisite?
Remedy,
closed.
Words, words;
define!
Incantation,
dissemination,
quantitative
non-pertinent calculation,
corrosiveness,
concoction,
gluttony;
there is no find
to the humor
found.

—NOTHING IS SETTLED

Everything sits waiting
and nothing issues but the readiness to believe;
the atmosphere is ripe, impressed as it is
with gift—
yet, nothing (not even the tactile adventitiousness of an
element pointing
toward this earth) may claim more authority;
this little one's mind is developed, and such is the state
of the world we form.

—OF THE NATURALLY HUMAN KIND

In line at the checkout, unperturbed by the holiday mixture,
by the uproar of a quiet purchase and an easy press through
the season's aisles,
I dish out funds, and it must be evident,
in this disharmony of spirit, and falsity of stance,
that I hurt.
There is no canceling the inner-pounce of continual humor,
and the constant noise and brazenness in the relevance
meted out.

The registered human tells me that a coupon
                one-aisle down is available—
I'm taken aback:
How could imbalance be mustered away by a
single interruption?
(The hurt hurts more,
and her kindness allows me to see that this hurt is not
of an inner-kind but of a naturally human kind—
that which usurps!)

—ON A CANDLE'S FLAME

The crash was never meant to be;
it lasted long into night—long into the seeping
of the dark's listless troll, this dying stars' insistence
on not balancing the state of things.
The smoke relished by the leftist mood advanced,
and within the hurt of metal,
in the cough of the engine's congested tune formed
                an aura of light

        dimly bright; it alluded
to the crying
of this paling lights' indulgence.
It was pure sense,
      like the sternness on a candle's flame.

—ON A CERTAIN SPECIES

There's a certain species that seeks its own

like a handle to a door.

It tools the mechanism, jars it open, and finds that
for which it searched…
                                    then robs it.

—ON OCCASION

On occasion,

deep in the evening's mist, by some river

long forgotten and long-since

abandoned,

I log all the mornings spent—

the times that might have been,

emptiness in the fullness of time,

love's occasional signs,

        half-spent and done.

They too search me out, but find me rock

tied to a mountain

beside a road without end.

—ON COATED LIGHT

The light

shines in the meadow

and falls

on the eye

like dust from a storm

in some June

far from memory—

a lost feeling.

—ON COLD NECESSITY

This morning congeals, ices to the rim,
and my long day's travels hang dutifully from the sky's
riffled edges;
    the sun sees them whole and smiles—if thinly.

I taste the searing cold,

but who in his right mind would venture to celebrate?

The undoing of ripe-fallen summer!

After I've pressed through the day's chores, I hope
to still be moving; foolish, perhaps—

    for necessity is my mead and glee.

—ON COMFORT ZONES

The comfort zone—

that need to be satisfied in skin, to be understood

too readily,

to be factored in as more than human.

Is it easier to descend into that fiber's freeze and halt someone else's form

than to bloom?

Is it easier to rest in the depths of heart and curb

someone else's urgency,

to have

than not have?

Coldness stretches through the catacombs of self none-too briefly

and demands harshly.

Would that we ruled our look and stopped this need.

—ON CONTINUAL TALK

Talk is irrelevant, and as the whimsies reveal,

fodder for the person's tongue, courage for the steal;

its continuance fosters audacity, in the communicant's voice

never quelling, always hovering

in temporal noise—

Listen, for the murmurs dawn,

and falsehood glistens

as step

furthers dance.

—ON CROSSING THAT LINE

I've crossed a line,
and yet—
I don't really have the courage to admit it.

I know I've done so,
but what's the efficacy in that?

Knowledge is a fine and delicate thing,
but in the final analysis,
it's just that: words on paper—
a prisoner's sentence seeking hope.

I don't see the crossing.

Even the guardian of my heart cuts back
        on the humor of it all.

I'm gifted with this sadness, worn
and pressed constantly.

Oh, actualization!
When will you thrill on the fact that seeks to be

fact?

ON CROWNS AND SUCH

What are these thorns made of?
There is a point to each one; each enters

the epidermal
as if it were non-human, as each is.

Each one casts a net upon it
with small stakes,

saying, "I know you,
and have known you from the beginning;

you lodge against a wall—
a weed pressing up

against a square
like a snake weaving through the building's eaves

never leaving done
what he has willed to start."

All of it is cordoned,
prettified, in doubts unsaid;

you might change, you say, and yet,
    still they pierce!

—ON DEAD WEIGHT

The barreling of a jet towards a parameter's goal

is easily made full by the forces needed to be overcome;

the beauty in the crash

is only met by the novelty's course,

and by the sight's enormity—

it is simply dead weight upon a ground filled
with more dead weight.

—ON DECISIONS

The left hand falsifies the times,
and the right bounces ajar—is taken aback.
The regiment is simple:
A decision has been made, but its ultimate end wavers,
to be tied to a past as if by nature damning;
this reservoir is not accustomed to lack.
      The dimple of the mix in the need savors
the truth it jams—
even the plausibility of the times
        returns in rhyme.

—ON ENDINGS

There's no waiting

for an ending that never comes,

nor is there a reason to be generous

when it does

as everything ties in well;

it makes no sense to be trudging

through the dying—

for when its arrival is counted,

no other need be found.

What is is,

and what never comes never was.

—ENDLESS JOURNEYS

Endless journeys:
There is no way to re-dedicate them, to fit these
measures of conscious time to form—

no remedy avails itself for the road-work needed,

                    and into this mix falls
the future always calling to be filled: a feature lifted
                    onto consummation.
All of this adds up quantitatively,

                    but comes short of the quality
searched for in this life—
It stands to reason that, as lives are meted out,

it's rare they find

the lawless law which rules the mind;
                    perhaps, they were never meant to.

—ON HABITS

A habit arises pressed for food and posits
      this hope:

If I remain keen to my surroundings
and try to understand
that my nourishment comes from ground
(or wood),
my fault may be found intact
though drought perform her good.

—ON LAYERED EYES

The clothes are in the dryer
edging toward an end; two minutes remaining, and the
spin's hold
mesmerizes:

The wings of the mockingbird's lust to free itself palls
        in the swing of the wind, churning as it does
over the whole of the earth.

All things capsize in these waves,
        ships on the high seas tossing up to the highest crest,
        again an attempt
at freedom and the easing of things.

A little over a minute (the revolution never ends),

only the trail of propaganda pulses,
inwardly, evenly balanced but shamelessly continuous,

like the Ferris wheel's airy touch, or the young boy's roll of
a tire
on a hot August eve as he's called by his mother for supper—

It's a holiday, and he's not listening, nor do
the layered eyes
of this lady who launders.

—ON LISTENING

Life, it must be lived—
By not living it, we label it breathless.

The consequence of a flower's fall never registers as
a flaw.

It is what it has given us that matters,

what it has shown us about ourselves that matters,

whether we see this or not which truly matters.

Yes, death is a rather barren quadrant to
mutter through—
and yes, it is mate to the man as if by template, a wife to
the living,
spouse to the grit of ongoing insurgency—

but the cues must be braced
and inculcated as such, must be registered by will
as documents of heart ready for use.

Consequences are of import to the whole as a whole,

and we, as parts thereof, must listen.

—ON MACHINES

The machine lies still
in the dark damp room like a covered sofa
never used, ever there, in time,
distanced from itself, from humanity's use—free.
An ad in the paper stirs its potential,
and its wires start to mingle with excitement,
spark with an obdurate wish
to be reeling with the notion that, again…
it will be roughly instituted, full of life, for time
                    is an issued show.

—ON MEETINGS

Meetings are nice, digging deeply into the
project, taking
the object

from the flame out of the vise,
and all the lies found
rejuvenate, bloom, rebound—

It is no surprise that the ruse in the logic
is seemingly distant, anagogic

(then comes the rise in the matrix, windingly wound as
it is

to its covered turn).

—ON NEEDS

Every now and then
these are wheeled in, bouncing about,
tested like basketballs in March, paddled up into the air
              for easy notice—
These might be cataloged as instruments,
curving around for knowledge, road-wise and weaving, to
a degree
weaving, and in times advanced,
but…

    journeys end;
these are then edified … in their heart's interior,
        captured—

        in warmth!

—ON NEW OPENINGS

What is the quiet to do

when its silence is bombarded by new stop…

non-existence, dangling hope?

There are no turns to be found in this world to melt
the turbulence
              of silent noise,

and when the references come,

they drive in like soft steel on a barren air—

The press of the atmosphere is too great to resist or measure.

What is the quiet to do but juggle in stability, forge up

into its cave like a thread unrolled?

—ON PRESUMING

The flesh, revitalized and youthful pulls us toward

the old way.

Into the inconsequential, we fall

at one with the ho-hum existence demanded of us—

the easy life!

A song reforms the memory.

A movie's rejoinder keeps us from stumbling.

A delicious meal calms us and sends us on our way—

I must presume

(and note, I am only presuming here!)

that we are only human, after all.

—HOWEVER LONG

However long the sun may wail,
the same you'll never sail—
you'll never long to meet it halfway there;
and who would want such range?
For timeless creatures never change this end
which circumstances share—
The depths will ring and store your many hopes within
and setbacks forward march;
on they'll form and rise, form and rise
these gems of sweet disguise
        onto the master's arch.

IN LIFE

In life,

you reach for your hat,
and of a sudden, the molecules are weaving,
very much like that thermostat in your car that, when it
is cold,
you're hardly ever
leaving.

THE TIMES ANSWERED

Funny how the times answer

to the movement of the atmosphere simply by

its tie to the radiance of the pugilist's entry into
the arena—

in his wish to play the customer.

Why?

—ON SWIVELING WHEELS

The swivel to a chair bars any noise,

traps the probable instance evolving; crickets harbor in
stunned silence, maimed

by the frequency of the roll in these purposeless wheels—on
the run!

It is the same with people caught by the toll of a bell,

peculiarly quiet before, non-eventfully still. Of a sudden, they
are moved, pulled into

action,

forced to make good on the turns indicated;

is someone torn mentally to the point of imbuing the atmo-
sphere quickly

with his non-befriending hand? Is there ... is there
a conclusion

looming?

And will the villain's notoriety part?

Swiveling wheels are quite harmless, quite in tune with the
jumps in this world

to quiet chatter—the swivels in the chatter, well,

                    that's another matter.

—ON THE BETTER REMEMBRANCE

>   At times we walk too sure, as when the breakage
>   and weld
> of iron is laid, for all time bedded;
> then comes the rustic leaf, which plays dumb and asks us
> to give.
>   What is kept for the future overwhelms,
>   too full to be honestly held,
> too fast-stopped and empty-headed to be reasonably brief—
>   Let the forgetting come,
>   the better remembrance ... live.

—ON THE FINALITY OF ELEGANCE

This degree of motion: To be well, radial to the times,

not be judged, to this instance roped, looped, to the solution's
outcome full—

when the elements counter the will, treat the conclusions
as fauna

in a limited jungle—
it is then that the sounds generated fail,
                    in the reeling of the moment fail,
            in the thickness of bungle fail.

This look through water, a merciless prong reaching for the
fiery light
                    of becoming—

Someone drops their eyes, sockets now
summing: appearance!

(Little is lengthened.) What is short is long in the catalog of a
day; tomorrow feeds

and thinks of its own accord—
                    but this is merely say.

—ON POINTS

The fourth posts west,
the other three east ... and yet,
their shades press north,

        but...

if the air should curve
like the Spanish stallion's desert jumps,
rise from the flow like an ease in the temperature
amid its groundless tests,
then I can avail myself to the elemental claim
that life may never be the same.

—ON THE GROUNDED FLIER

The reach is always long;
into the depths of resistance twists its seed,
past its ornamental existence
on toward its sturdy remembrance

and a long-lost memory.

It soars among the clouds
like a wide-winged bird searching for prey,

clear-eyed and pointed,
but disliked by the foreign species,

for when it slides
it veers as another kind of creature:

a slithering rover above groundless attachment;
the heat is immense.

I know of no other entity
so oblong and non-square of feature

that mutters through the grind so fearless,
and then, at seizure,
so non-being.

—ON THE HARBOR'S HOLD

The harbor holds my heart
like an easy pool of smooth-worn tissue, apart
from the pages shoring up nights;
the sandy water enhances itself onto the keel
of my little journeyer; the mooring lights
have settled into distance,
                    and an easy feel
calls me up. Its hull is now a ginger blue and its interior white
set for change. If by chance the weather lessens,
and the morning fog rises, the brief sight
in this pushed-for zeal
may fray its edges for an easy meal.

—ON THE HISTORY OF
FINE ILLUSIONS

There is a comfort in knowing

the order of ease, which drops from the heart

when the chains have loosened; sinews reverberate

apart from the sternly shaped back

like sweet water on a noon day, and that morning (long-
ago lost)

pushes to be gained once again,

in memories braced as if by osmotic fuel, and at no cost.

The noises of this world cater less emphatically,

toss through this vengeance for their own right to be

no more,

and relinquish their conversant waves

from the cresting of many seas.

I must say,

these fine illusions still dance,

but in another time and in varied frame

(so too, as a different glance).

—ON THE HUNG TREE

The hurt smiles,

impedes our path as if it were a dying journey,

a reluctant end; it rushes into the length

of long extension,

and scourges to the point of emptiness—

the evening's day holds to be risen,

to be shining.

Laurels turn into the briar's pointed limb

and round into a crown;

they symptomatically actualize.

We carry this burden,

hang on its justice,

weigh in its knowledge,

understand its death—

a hung tree bars none from the suddenness

of ecstasy.

—ON THE INVISIBILITY OF WALLS

The ground never gives up her secrets,
little is allowed by way of prayer—
it need not be pried into,
but if so, it may choose to deter the dig.

Some of us of a relentless nature feel obliged
to sink into its form,
scientists endlessly searching;
it is not enough to know its name,
to sense where it will strike next, or fall into its aura
of hegemony.
                    Its pull

            (basically understood,
it must turn to resolving what it has set out to find:
            the meaningful solution).

This ground is hallowed,
its system given,
and it is always the returning
that pushes the issue;
the walls have been raised
(however invisible they may be).

—ON THE SCENE

It was in the opening
I saw her, in the shell she placed
before me,
all within her proximity,
in this deep ravine bounded by steep hills—
her streams,
the comforts of her home abandoned.

　　She tarried,
and then, in her favor, noticed me; it …
startled:
this soul's notion longing
for a faraway place.

—ON THE SEAMLESS WORD

The word is seamless
when it comes to moving illogically;
it stammers long and loose
as it seeks to strain the gnat;

           to impress so
is to besiege the fortress completely, to raze
the structure fully
and then attend the win, the conqueror
        established.

This never stops;
it's as if the central crux of the thing
never arrives, the outer boundaries walling all
that wills to succeed—
and yet, this movement is there,
       offering its outlet,
       edging toward conclusion.

ON THE WRONGNESS...

Weapons are easily worn

by the warrior who has hiddenly sworn

not to worry prodigiously long

on the wrongness of song.

—ON WHOM...

On whom falls the ax

when the candle's alarming issue

eschews its own light?

On her whom no one will tax

owing to her petulant tissue

per dwindling night!

A BOUNCING KITE

It's all the same—

this passing through that part-world eye

as a knowledgeable kite;

though it may bounce without blame

like a bird past a postulant's wizardly sky,

it will never bite.

—ON UNITIES

Living in departments,
moving through his sections like a squirrel,
in his not finding, adamant,
trailing past some terminal ending in tomorrow,
worrying his way into the new,
finding his being numbed, from a past too worked
and worn,
irrelevant to the times...
This mode of being tends to rule against what works
coming from a whole, which tended toward
        the more profound unity.

—ON VOWELS AND MEN

"And the vowels of men pull through the maze as parables veer

through the thoughtless; from these

come sequences formless, towers babbling form,

stuttering foolish insignificance;

on will the two, these men and their call,

racing for that wish to be where no encumbrance

may wishfully fall."

THE BRIEF SPARK!

Its legs are wiry, freely moving;
maneuvering the ground like a tool in an assembly line

guarding its back from the task at hand
and working to perfection.

It sees me and stands erect, a statue to the eye,
seemingly camouflaged.

Its limbs align with the floor,
and its eyes are reflecting like dust.

It thinks I don't see it, still as it is,
of its rock stance sure.

My shoe is simple and flat; it slaps well flimsiness,
but the air about it is just as alive.

Its surrounding cushion breaks,
warning it of danger.

Quickly, it flies off like a chaparral cock
to the outer banks of this home's interior walls.

I'm amazed at its slipperiness.

—ON WINE SKINS

His resolute juncture
stops—
that which
has taken a backseat,
now roughly darkened
in the shadows
of an ongoing presentation,
wishes to be known,
to be remembered,
reworked...
He sees himself
harshly

treated, ease
          withheld
by the new.

And he shows it,
fears too quickly, pauses;
upon seeing this vision,
he is himself
assured,
yet, he waddles forth.
Wine skins seek looseness,
now that old leather
cools.

ONLY THE NEW NEED
REARRANGING

The shades move slowly,
quietly succumbing to the day.
The doors open and the first comers
parade in; the troops are ready, filled as they are
with the courtesy of good fortune.
No easy fortress, this sales-place where
money is exchanged
and only the new need rearranging.

The smiles are plenty,
in good form today, and the dollar bill
reflects a murky green light
shadier than the shades that allowed light in.
These customers have no need to move
but to simply stop restraint,
for if money is exchanged,
only the new need rearranging.

—OPENING UP

What if nothing follows,

nothing erupts,

nothing frees itself for the shine to come,

for those quips

full of that crescent sound?

Versification toddles in its scamp

    through wet grass.

It crawls meagerly through the swallow
of quietude,

mouths limp,

terse with their halo of fortitude,

stern in their stalwartness.

Ten minutes is a long time for roses to stammer.

(Fifteen minutes has them walking

onto a new product.)

—OR NOT!

First, she'll spill through the mill like an ant,

say she might when she can't,

then test the water's tepidness for rise

first seen in her eyes.

It's simple arithmetic to me—

the lynch pin in the screeching calliope—

and just as the soup's fine aroma catches,

so does her heart when it latches.

For, every woman wants to be won—

even if it's by some modern-day Rashomon,
    or not—

it's all dependent on the spot!

—OVERFLOWING TEARS

The windows are up, the wind still,

matter strangely melts in the heat; I know
what's coming:

the skies sober, none is calmer than the sound of the
rustling oak.

Suddenly, an anger mounts … and falls like a petal from
a rose;

windows close, and the flower's aura reflects

on the non-tearful ground below.

PAPER BENDS

Paper bends—

set as it is on a table that doesn't;

a pencil writes, and its carbon points to a rule of thumb.

(What is written can be worked over, its language changing to fit the times—

      even when the times don't matter.)

These sounds will always be with us, prowling through freedom:

         the price of play for the living day.

—PAPER THOUGHTS

Paper shines too well—
rarely crimps when you want it to.

When you desire its demise,
its reflection somehow dissolves this notion and lures

you into salvaging its grace,
and when the times are aesthetically robust,

when the need arises,
what happens?

The must in the force comes,
and your hands are tied to pushing the envelope,

to re-instituting life,
and not relegating this piece of wood

to the nether regions. Is it understood?
You see this,

and you move toward this;
you do not desist

and okay its presence
on the table top.

Illusions to a T...

so is the strength of the tabled oak
to the ends you see.

—PERHAPS

A person sits

        never moving, never uttering a word,
waiting, waiting.

For what,
      with a grocery basket full of myriad items—
           pieces of matter this individual will
           never use?

Buses pass and never stop;
they shower their emblem of meaning,
but never stop;

      Next time!

A restaurant sits in front, but only stares run through it, as if it
weren't there;
      its many windows allow peering, but no…

There's

              no desire.

I dare not ask if everything's okay;
I dare not ask if the day is too hot to be sitting there.

I dare not ask how the day's going,
or where home is...

I wonder who sits there now.

... perhaps, this is me;
    perhaps... perhaps, this is you...

PRE-LENT

"Her hair descends in a stream of lilac shimmer;
it is pre-Lent in the deeper valley.
Every word she speaks is draped in violet rainbow like the
rain's un-dished color
                    to the sun's untinged sally.

I matter less; only the depths set me free.
This is tryst, and I amble for that breath that might
be sea-bred.
But ... what is this resonance coming from the sky's expanse?
And what sits firmly at my side so basely led?"

A pull restrains me,
and through the valley presses onto its azure cool.
I would require a remedy
but am no fool!

I call to her who would be mine,
to return to save me from my starved intrusion;
she comes in the prime of death with all its warmth laid up,

other-worldly and beyond this world's illusion.
And so, my evening's end is spent,
                as I tell this tale newly gone—
                pre-Lent."

—"PRICELESS"

Coming attractions were given:

"To those who wish as the child,
you shall know no boundaries, and the works
of your thoughts will flow—
as butterflies or small birds, for nectar, flow.
From the bough the view will be grand,
simple, yet saturated with imaginative terrain
as clear as the blue sky seen.
No directions shall plunder your dreams,
nor will there be obstacles to cross,
and the edges of time will saunter before the gates
of a fold not yet through—
                 priceless!"

—QUICKNESS

Quickness steps into the mix
like a fire waltzing through the evening's celebration,
taking the joy from the whole into the part
far from the specifics of the condition—
voices
salute its efforts,
but no calliope can be heard.
incumbent laughter roams, resolving nothing—
            a severe study.

—QUIET AS ILLUSION

Quiet as illusion!

It sends you out of a place,

which exists as an intolerable truth

and quickens the heart

when its need arises.

    (Every trace

of its cover wheels in!)

This easy semblance of mind revolves

around a center,

and we may be excused

if sorrow tears away from it all,

but not for long.

(Still,

the bumps in the road can be heard

pounding upon a path

long gone.)

—WATCHER OF THE LIGHT

From the morning's rising ache,
when these bones deride my place and stamp me
with the lapsing time which bids me sleep
and never wake,
I hold to all you've given—
to the noon-day's charm that meets me small
and saddles me with inconstancy,
forever showing me the crudeness of a lie that bounces
off the twilight's wall.
I hold to all you've given—
into the evening's breached rite
of long-lost happenings never found, or thanks
once hoped for but never fully made
in the quiet shade of night.
To this darkest day too nigh uneven,
O ever-present Watcher of the light,
I hold to all you are,
and hold to all you've given.

—THE RED

Red's color:

brighter than the red

it's made of,

this meddled stuff,

muddling

through years of wear.

This wanting

(and not wanting)

form,

through rise and fall,

now encroached upon us,

instituted,

finding us well,

(at times)

this spilled red—

this outlet

of escape.

—REFINISHING

She figured on celebrating, stapling her roster of vices onto

the main of her life by taking over the room;

she would remake it to fit the hurt within and envision herself
coming to terms with it.

And so, a banner emerged,

hung from the ceiling calling for a movement of heart—

a re-establishing of the ready flavor of love non-loved; a
portrait of demise

plunged from the wall like a hidden safe readily zoned, the
carpet stifled in red,

in puffiness, in easy assessment, in reference...

                              She closed the door,

re-opened it to find herself surprised,

and then closed it again.

RIFT

The lesson learned upon waking,
on finding out life gives me no choice but to live,
escapes me;
I'm settled with the notion
that brightens no day,
that tosses all the throws into the bin
and lets loose the dogs of war.
I see the sun
but find no solace in it,
see the greening grass,
its blooming splendor all around me,
and yet harbor
no resistance to the fall I feel in my heart over the
resonating call
to be more
than I might have been.
The answers are there, and they stand me up;
I rise faultily,
indigently,
quietly resolved not to stand
and fight this steely frame of mind
now mowing through this day,
now rift
to all that I was.

—ROADS?

Roads?
Made to step easily through when matter toils?
Even when they melt into the system?
                        Like a word stated,
            quickly forgotten?
Like a cloud just as quickly stultified
by an ultra-sensitive wind and an unforgiving sun?

(Beginnings are just as simple;
they forge ahead black, like pieces of coal stepped on by time
yet fitting into the middle way like plains
barren to the world and open
                    as to distance.
Once at their end, the life force notices and turns—
a pattern is given.)

The roads we walk meet wittingly
but never truly;
they are as objectively short on substance as they are long—
a disappearing species moving forward
        by its own subjectivity; alas
            this was meant to be!

—SANCTIONING NESTS

My love is a given (even if it is tossed in with this rock
and its turbulent cumbersome visual, which marks all
of life—
though with you in its cleft it is less than usual); the weather-
man's cast
is lost to your beauty's harsh winter day
as is the earthquake, which brandishes the non-usurped
ground at its edge;
to my mind it lightly languishes like a mockingbird's warble.
The turning of wind in this constancy changes my world,
holds in its tracks like a drop from a tear erupting
from the silence of heaven.
I praise your involvement in this joviality, in this rest,
and with diligence, I sanction its nest.

—SIMMERING

Just sitting—
in a warm library...
sitting,
waxing interest,
loosely thinking
about...
writing: a poem? Essay?
Something.

The clicking of another computer pierces
the air, fingers figuring paths,
as my own do.

I'm thinking again...
     thinking.

The cool of the morning's brisk wind doesn't
pull here;
the rush of the traffic simmers
to a stall
     here, but then
(in a small town) little vaults out. Everything
simmers here.

Someone walks in, asks about the holidays,
shadows a book, checks it out,
leaves,

and matter does not move beyond its act
of moving—
               no single entity dares to.
Not even the dust evokes a cry.

       I'll write little today.
After I...

dare to not do anything.

THE BLUEBIRD

It stands quiet in its domain—
in the stellar part of the universe, apart and distant,
arbiter which it is on the state of the world.
(It sings,
and it calls,
and then
scurries away
onto the perfect edge
       of day.)

—WALTZING WIND

Waltzing wind,
    weathering little that comes,
dawning upon the heads of those who never die,
trekking through the fullness of death
        beyond the given lie,
    never overwhelmed,
dancing like a stem upon an earth never free—
and never saddened
        by the suddenness of eternity—
    weaving in the noon-day sun.
Weaver of noose-like charm donning onto turn
for we who kill,
        and never ever burn,
        the crux in the thing—
the thing in the slice we live, piece of our heart.

Waltzing wind, we who are elsewhere will not
    from you forever part.

—THE DOGS OF WAR

Their skin is triangular, coated in mesh,

strung over war—

like the mindset hovering over the listless;

their acts are singular   like the fallen,

or the terrain of a star—

caught. And the western shore sings,

metallically,

for their form now changes. We are

this matter's coat bought.

—THE PITCH!

<u>At the game</u>:

"His view winds up;
his pitch is a little to the right, too lame.
His aim is for a much higher norm,
expected—

The ump sleeps.

The would-be batters, his opponents,
regulate, for depth's sake.

The song's in
but soon forgotten.

He lies,

ready for his second strike;

his fans are thrilled!"

(But the Lincoln-like winner's cloned smile halts.)

—OUR PRESENT STATUS

"Branches filter through the sun's bright glare

and shelve all matter not grown of root and
sinewy chlorophyll—

not touched by the dewy wet glimmer of leaves

clung to root."

A referee is needed for this world:

to erase the mind's eye, establish a claw to take from the
vision's changing aura,

and deprive the judge of substance; let him wrong the wrong

no wrong can right...

                    and turn away.

—THE FIGHT

A hum streams through the floor like a fog searching;

it slides into the vestibules of numb pride,

hidden by lower achievement.

Above the fray of fine-swept floor,

grass-wet minds lower toward the lowest word.

From the bottom shelf, close to the unknown and
non-looked for,

a machine tools quietly to the newness of time.

—The Jabbok waits.

—THE FLAME

History moves

but lessens to a faulty degree

and reminisces in the dark

for society.

She cools in bright wild circumference,

in dotted file,

and never averts her gaze,

or her maudlin smile.

She descends as thick mud

from her varied days,

then turns her sweeter stare

to the flame of distant ways.

THE GAZE!

Her eyes threaten
and undermine the set upon which the future
lures those souls not yet founded—not yet predicated
to this world's vile cure.
It's just a look, and yet it warms no part, calms
no storm,
fails no fire which nears the heart
(too near her view
to be something other than partial game).
This gaze enriches none who might weave through
(as if it were industrial in its turning curve,
like a fearless enforcer churning past
        by senseless nerve).

We hear her footsteps, trained and burning high;
we stir and strain and step through netted
        sigh.

THE HOMELESS ODE—

Longing for the future that must never come,

in an instant gone, and in half that time resurfaced—

its ramifications prime, manifested sun.

I shall be revealed as a man untimely formed, and this society,

in its bright elusive cloth, and in its ways upper-scaled,

shall rise and brace as wall without the mask

              and risk disguise.

I fear for myself in this undoing, in this non-fashioning,

and yet, I must advance, though heaven knows why.

I shall not return to rest like hung meat.

I shall live the fumes, bereft of lies, in a vacuum,

              harder then and most unwise!

THE INTERLOPER

It is a matter of course
when an interloper notes the worse,

in his circumstances' scene
what he might surreptitiously curse

from this happening's right (now clear)
is his freedom from fear.

His need to proceed untrammeled, sure
of his presence (so near),

he stops at no measure and stirs
far beyond the world's

reverence for the changes that mend.
Has he his oyster's pearls?

(We must adjure
that he has surely met his cure.)

—THE INVENTION

She walks on a road not quite wide,
as if freely unleashed;

far from wonder falls insistence at her side,
embarked on a plan not yet cinched.

Neither heat nor cold cushions intention,
as she covers her headless scheme;

though this be not invention,
we rule it is invention following dream.

Questions abound:
her wish to be fully understood?

Not sound
(more like motionless wood).

—THE KING AND THE RING

The dying king said nothing

in his last wish to be silent and unwieldy.

His friend gazed intently and simply took the ring
from his right hand for safekeeping.

It was then readied for the new fit,

but the holding bin was found to be filled

with another five rings.

Being that the present large one

might find it difficult keeping there,

the question arose:

Should the share in the changing storm wait

for the seventh ring and a quake-less fate?

THE MELT IN THE FIRE

1

My eyes falter in the morning hours;
they praise their age as if age were an end to be praised.
I open the door and feel the cool on my face.
These eyes see, but in a blurry fade ...
among the flowers placed (as if my powers were planted,
rising slowly, a painting for the painter becoming).
The mornings are minimally low, lowly,
                and they grow impatient, shameless—
It's the latter these eyes see, volumes spoken quickly!

2

        The hound hounds;
through the years he has passed me fondly, yet fast and still ...
moving but only in a wanting sort of way.
The easy flame falls, the melt in the fire stays.

—THE MESSAGE IN FULL

"Hold on to the line," says the tender shoot
as the ground gives way

to the grasses above, in through the system, in
and through
the aftermath given trails this message in full.

It has no relevance to growth, only to surety in its
understood say,
and the grub in the centerline's tub traces up.

Then, from above, an ant circumvents the field;
its attempts

to stop the eagerness learned,
                impressed.
                        "Hold on to the line,"

whispers the tender shoot as the ground
gives way to the grasses above.

(And in through the system, in and through
the aftermath given trails this message in full.)

— THE GOODNESS
OF LOSS!

A pause—
from the passages found—
comes
for the check
on the goodness of loss!

On the now-open ground,
matter is sought,
and
in the interim,
integrity's caught.

It isn't older than the new,
yet
the future wills to extricate
the fixed sight:
"Away
with the variable light!"
　　　Away.

Averse to present venues …
this is the point—
the saying which bothers
the table—quick to delay
and to label
　　　the less able.

—THE ONE BEFORE ME

The goal hasn't changed, nor has the will to see
it through;

It is still laden in fevered thoughts—
        dated to memories past.

The turn hasn't arrived—
hasn't seen the weakness in the constancy surround-
ing matter.

            An outgrowth...
            The simple idea needs to feel free,
to stand on its own, away from the long-saturated
pummel of rain,
never sinking deeper than the sun allows.
                    I can see...
            This desert forms

even as I sense the reason for its essence,

yet it climbs empty.

This isn't the road I meant to take.

There was a time when bravery glued to me like a
done deal...
Now, there is no other before me
        but the one before me.

THE PARDONABLE SIN

There is an uneasy but pardonable sin vaulting onto the push
towards life! In its razor-sharp insistence, it holds onto habit,
surreal-like, pursuant on a path,
ever hovering before us as a circular cloud hovers, dances,
past our future,
a buoy onto land, unfriendly at best...
It jars every fiber of our hearts into a place
and caresses the ligaments like a pull to the depths, furthering
the work,
bargaining with no one as it feels its way into the world.
The storms evoked by this insurgency cannot hold—
or so we think. The matter re-evaluates itself, and on the road,
seeks resolution.
Long before this dance has swirled away into the distance,
taking with it the semblance of lived reality, experienced,
briefly renovated,
the returning spin begins again,
and onto the shores of a wide and barren ease we land.
They tell me life preservers help, but...

—THE POET'S THROW

The curve swerves in the throw,
and the winds pass (drawn as they are to the quickness
of the stellar whim they wield); the dot that stands
alone need not last,
no longer sail on toward its portal's count.
A smaller light may veer,
and (in the mix of night and day) fire less Promethean
than its zeal
to shore its incandescence. The rocks
empty, yet hold too well wide-short of this non-
targeted seal.
Arched above this whole expanse is a branded immen-
sity flailing like a star,
stumped to cloudless eaves.
        Poets once were wont to gently trek
the long remains of steel-cast walls, but rounded now as
they are,
they pleasurably lay by heaven's row, at war ... at war.

—THE PROWL

Winding through the sand like a lion on the prowl, he
weaves …
mane higher than the blades of grass; the dew tallies up and
his follicles rave

and press to the sky. To a dance is this feline stamped.
He stops, and the air symbolically holds in its route—
its itinerary
                              broken.

There is no wind to talk of, no other jungle quadruped to
bother with—to tangle
and oppose him. He sees his destination and aims for it like
the leopard

                              he's obviously kin to.

A lizard purrs to a tree and innocently sallies about

                  To his task at hand, the cat moves.

Into a sail spreads the wind; the grass pulls to the sides
(so as not to get crunched, as if this were possible).

The catch is clawed, and clawed again,
then loosed (as if he were playing with it).

His eyes, these
piercing ornaments
on a well-lit branch

brace; again, he claws, and plays it for the fool that it is.

Finally, it's held in his mouth, and it's done.

The stage is bright again—the dance ended—and the players
get the standing ovation they deserve; what an opening night!
A few things
might have been developed better, and yet ...
well...

However well you cut it, it's well cut.

—THE RAIN KEEPS ON FALLING

She fades into the limelight

like an astrophysicist fades into his numbers,

dangling from the premises of time

like an underrated axiom from a long-ago theory.

The work has been tooled through

and the service to mankind established.

Only the semblance of a runaway mind languishes now,

and the rain keeps on falling.

THE REASON I SING

The ease with which we've walked
in the early morning hour is vaguely remembered
as the setting sun recedes,
              and the humor
of these days is forgotten, tossed into the bin of lost bits
and a memorable fog.

The walk to school is nothing but cold to the eye;

warm cookies in the oven are relegated to an outer twinkling,

and the people whom we once parted with
are distantly recessed, summarily erased and done with.
They have lounged on after life and lived,
but pressed onto the maze of a world long disturbed,
barely won.

        No issue with the past to find,
           nor relevance to the meaning there lost,

yet hope reaches out onto their doorstep
with the gifts they bring.

        For this reason, I sing.

—THE RISING SUN

The rising sun,
so ran the evening's thought,
    establishes what was once stapled
to the bottom of an ocean not yet dry, and brings it up
to be scattered about;
it hopes to bewilder the frame
upon which nothing mates, but the climb
        for remedy.

This wish,
to be freer than the sun,
is institutional
in its way/state.
It now rises in the dark
of light, dimming
into the morning's brine
censoring no more,
to be sold for less
in time.

—THE SHADES THE SHADOWS FOOL

(The sun longs to weave, like the night,
to rise and to rule,
and the light lengthens; no bulbs turn,
and shades
     the shadows fool.)
Nothing in March connects;
its early spring song tags onto time
     too wrong.

(The sun longs to weave, like the night,
to rise and to rule,
and the light lengthens; no bulbs turn,
and shades
     the shadows fool.)
Daylight time ministers
to wellness—nudges and strives
     to inform.

(The sun longs to weave, like the night,
to rise and to rule,
and the light lengthens; no bulbs turn,
and shades
     the shadows fool.)

—THE SEVENTY-TWO

My thermometer says seventy-two degrees,
but the feel is foreign,
and the air crawls jauntily to its present humor and its
set heat;
the breeze counters the crustiness—stops it cold:
    "This is winter, my friend, and in the short run
only your sternness embraces my un-embraceable sun;
you may wallow in witness today,
but not long in my bold-buried blur. Away ... away, I say,
for the feel of your air derails thought,
and your ventures jolt naught."
Winter too proses his time with his elegant maze,
and cries:
    "My friend, you're in a daze,
in your solidity fooled, in your presence long-stopped;
the season's all mine.
                Let's say you're cupped.
I lower degrees as to my company's right,
        colder today [even colder tonight]."
And would a body portion its physical time and pain,
dance to the age with its variable lance?
    "You've aged, dear one, by many a year;
long have I been adding time to fear.
Ten more degrees I envision you'll feel, and ten more before
            you unyoke its final door."
And this is the state of the seventy-two
         [then undaunted and bold],
now caved canvassing cold.

—THE STATE OF THE SOUL

An island waiting,

sparkling with unlit favor,

in the fullness of being, in the smallest of spaces,

vibrancy in stasis,

and in consequential circumstances wooed,

in a market of its own;

old, written,

a star newly bursting,

and with the right liquid brushed,

dot engendering rhythm,

dance,

a rock gliding, into the universe riding,

into the universe riding...

...LIKE SUMMER SNOWS

In the cool of sweet autumn,
as this race for icy mail descends, I grieve,
for within her heart's incursions ease—
            lows give.
Still, the dint of flow, from this fine stream
and its pebbled fall, resounds within
as a cooling gift from heaven's gate to me;
my sights are many and varied are the caps I see.
They gently tip of surety ...
        like summer snows to me.

—THE VIOLENCE OF CHANGE

Walking the way

tosses like a maelstrom from the skies,

logs like a stranger to the new,

and never pauses to breathe; no remedy
evolves from

this entity's resurgence,

for when she tools the door to the
gifted room

and jams the lock,

no understanding forms, little converts.

Turns come and go,

new opportunities advance.

This is the muttering tune that
trumps change—

always in the wings, her entrance there,

part-substance, part-instituted condition, and in no matter

relevant.

O, Change!

Change without havoc!

Heaven is at hand, but violence is its mean.

—TO THE BINS!

Trees are fine in their own little space,
easily looked upon,
stored to mind as pretty, very much in place,
to heart taken,
braced and sanctified …

but soon
the trimmers come with tools out; the scene
is re-evaluated.
Palms go.
The flowering red bush too.
All bow to the trimmer's steel
as they once bowed to the ground.
No words are said.

We accept the transformation and never blink—

These things,
like all things, must leave us
dead in their tracks—
leave us for the more formidable ways of man,
the newer man founded by man!

The rest? To the bins!
To the turning ground pressed.

A COLUMN...

A column
should never pulse solemn,
and the memory of its violence
should never waiver—
    a falling silence,
in time,
never asks to understand such rhyme.

THE WAYWARD EYE!

The crust,

in the making of deed and trust,

relinquishes swirl;

the cold view, never bounded by history,

ties mystery

to the simple world.

—TO DANCE REPEALED

The halls of justice trail in the mix

of curves and tricks—toss in the coarseness of the times,

newly founded; these pores open unfitted as they are in
their attachment—

quaintly placed. These halls groan on an easy ramp of good,

past the colors of a time unknown.

The new is quietly surmounted, in this sand never re-
evaluated, lain as it is

disengaged from the chain; yes, it is restructured
and cataloged

according to the present state of things, and ...

this "newness" sticks for a time but rebounds upon itself,
never taking hold,

never settling. The cracks, these splices in the road,

grow and reflect onto a being that will never stand. Pot holes

are easily covered, and for a two-week period or so, act as
if healed.

It's best to dance repealed.

—I'VE BEEN SMALL MANY TIMES

I've been small many times,
literally dwarfed beyond my means constantly.

At times like this, I stand alone and off,
like a clock un-rocked by the need to be correct, or a dance

timed by little form.
In my place, there's found the crucial remedy: a path

which leads me quietly out—
an un-interrupted surrogate ready at hand.

My own being in turmoil reaches for the difficult and rectifies
what has been manifested; it revolves, involves and turns

into the upward stem it should have grown into.
The small is seeded to stand as lost.

—TOO OLD

The river
rises;
it engulfs the edges
of this
swamp
as it reaches into
the roll
of the raking
opening
to the bay.

Our skiff
falters in turn,
bows off,
teeming in and
over
the waves
as it
seeks to rush
into
the depths.

Slowly,
the skies calm
and
the inkling
in the storm
leaves

its harsh bellow
to smile
on the journey
beyond;
we amble
like two
sailors
winding round a tanker,

too old to
be free
and
too old
to be right.

—TOO SOON

It was a swing,
a passion pulled fast,
like a broken limb
un-cast.

I sought to run
full force to an end;
I was stopped, parceled
by the bend.

No room for money,
fast choice,
too soon advanced,
reverts to noise.

—HOW DOES ONE PROCEED?

The reading jars the look,

and the waters stay the same long after the crossing;

it's a bridge—a transitional pleasantness

on a short leash and a terminal ending, like the breath I will
one day take

and from which I will never return.

This square box that carries one to its destination resumes

with a new client in its sights—a new mark

unbraced and unaware; all he knows is that one thing is whole

and will one day end, and that the other too lives whole,

though unknowingly so.

I know the ride is evident and real,

but after the vehicle has left the ramp and goodbyes are
in order,

how does one proceed to tour the border?

—UNTIL HER CROSSES
ARE CROSSED!

She was a wonder to her generation,
a statue for all to mimic and revolve around
as to an island deep in the Australian outback, on the reefs
of quiet reference and understanding glee,
overall, an understated emblem on a towered
edifice plaintively
bolstered by an out-of-the-way wall made from chain.
The light burned without burning and she saw without seeing
and pressed her mandates madly over her maidenly form
like a mermaid's hegemonic lure for passing ships—
she who clasps onto sternness;
what is seen is simple, but what is envisioned rises only
from the take in the mindset of the listener.
All is touted as joyous, wonderfully wonderful,
until her crosses are crossed.

—UP FROM THE DEPTHS

From the depths
of an early morning's dry rain,
and into the reefs of an ocean of guilt sun-drenched
in easy stone and crushed by thoughts unfolding
from the centers of an unruled welcome (now tainted
by whim
and a trust-less fodder),
I run through the claim that trots on a jungle filled with
edges sharper than the pointed ideas thought.
The whole is resolved by simply resting on a cheer
not there—
none of it matters in the scheme
    now braised,
caked as it is with a past overwhelming
in its senseless gearing towards a goal narrow
and much too slim to be judged as a win;
I may wail,

    but to no avail.

—WALKING GINGERLY

Walking gingerly,
millipede-like
in a slow maneuvering weave;
it is still ahead,
this overture with life,
still in embarkation
and full of verve—
I'm still on two.
(In this last
I search firmly
like the woman who stopped
to raze her floor
in her bid
for the coin she had lost;
it's sad
to be felt as if
on the outside—
    tossed.)

WE HOPE AND WISH

On the awful side of the board, not knowing when
to move and where you're bound—

no inkling as to the dimension of the path, or the color
of the distance harboring the pain of old age.

Yes, there is movement, but it's harried and dry,
non-evolving and stupid!

Still, the petals of the chrysanthemum bloom,
the dew

from her shoulders fall,
and the rustle

of the chameleon's shadowy extensions strew
through the wet summery grass.

I can see, if partly, why the birds swarm and nest,
why the trees tower low in the meadows,

why my species holds its own among the many:
We hope and wish.

WE'RE ON TO YOU

Why is it so dark mornings?
Is it because we've done something wrong?

Has the heart's palate dried?
Have the colors stuck like muscles to the watery depths?

Have we been out of touch?
Have those drums pounding in our ears loosened,

torn as they are from the truth now settling?
How is it we breathe in makeshift water?

Does this lend to darkness?
Or does that morning taper inwardly

like the deacon who sees his holiday leads into
this week's sermon?

I've seen the stars less glimmering,
seen them blink as if to say:

We're on to you, you who thought the world
was yours!

We're on to you, to you, to you!

WHAT IS THIS MADNESS?

What is this madness
forming in the distance, like a reflection
to a semblance, or likeness
in the country which surrounds us?
It pronounces the time as past and of no use as a
program ...
still, it wishes to perform
as if it were alive, bustling with an understanding feel,
with the ebullience of a forgotten aura;
I must admit that the instance
     succumbs to the unanswerable.

—WHAT TO DO

Knowledge is given to us for the asking;
the avenues in our quest for any solution are delivered
by many routes, two of which may fair best
over much lesser paths,
but even here, when the situation seeks finality,
when surety is impressed upon us,
    both helps founder.
The numbers let us down—algebraically as well
as descriptively;
the first measure takes us across a universe wide
with easy access to the answers needed as point by
point our colors
are placed to canvas.
Then comes note following note;
the breach arrives like a weed on a desert dune.
When the next dialogue descends (the descrip-
tive one),
the same occurs;
the stops are unhampered and sure, restful,
    (if uninvited).
        What to do?
The first thing is to stand up.
The next? To find something in the sun
which is not numbered and won.

WHAT WAS SAID

What was it that I said?
It was volatile and irreverent—caustic even;
it was doused in flames even before the fires started,
and was found trudging through the mire of accepted stability
and form
even as it foundered in the haven of my mind.
It was said—now it is done,
yet ... these ashes trail me like the dust of a tomb ever open
and still feel very much alive!

—WHEN DARKNESS COMES

If one has been too long in the verified light,

one forgets that it gets dark

when darkness comes!

—WHEN I'M ME

Maybe the days
wash away
only when the white sky
     melts.

Maybe the nights
shine
when the dark clouds
     see.

Maybe the times
settle
when the times
     change!

Maybe these tidbits
mean—
(only)
     when I'm me.

—WHERE I HOPE TO LAND

There lies a station found on the outskirts of the city;
it stands affronted by the dis-interested, by-passed even
by ruffians;
the woods lay hollow, panes prying into depths of forgotten
wonder, and the trees
align to this building's walls seamless to the sky
and just as awkward in their reach—
The winds hold their shattered smiles for her eaves.
Her wood encroaches on the turned-up limbs of air; she's
edged away.

And the peeling print of logo-battered light presses
and weaves
through the see-worn eyes of its own precious movement, as
the ground grins
leaning against her stumps,
laughing at the hallowed rim of her rolling lumps, held as
they are
so casually by the unreasonableness of time.

I stop to see
these shutters roll
on days off, and days on, and soon,
as if held by a second hand to the rail of the wood,

                    I understand ...
where I've been ...
              and where I hope to land.

—WHILE WE'RE SMILING

Irrelevant death!
I for one have never seen such an instance,
and if I had would have shuddered
having known my own demise might well
be ordered
to its vein—
short horizons soldered
by the breath's entailing fill,
by occurrence's number in its non-perturb-
ing dial—
none of us,
forsaken,
and when those last words are uttered,
may say, *it is done,*
and smile.

—WISHING WELLS AND PENNIES!

The wishing wells are all dry this year,

too long on the main, I fear—

too long in the hands of the frivolous to be grasped again

       as full and rich [as in past ages].

Pennies are thrown, and thoughts are paraded past them, but hope is lost,

to the edges of time relegated,

to the eternal onslaught of perambulated presence tossed,

by its smile

recessed onto the non-living waters of neutral earth!

What is now seen is stillness,

colorful monuments to the splendor of time

       recalled—

my pennies have stretched the breaking point.

They are now printed pasts.

A MEMORY LONG GONE

A table is set,
the cleanest slate available;
it could not be cleaner.

However, it is ruled, separated into eight pieces,

and a turquoise hue stands out,
but only barely—

the message will still arrive,
and the clock is set.

A worker enters; she is amazed.
The department rises.

She centralizes herself upon her square,
rectangular in size—

she sees that the seven others pale;
she fosters compassion

as a sibling might.

Done.
The others arrive,

to little note and a memory
          long gone.

—A SEARING QUIET

1

This wind terrified,
and the manner of wind
trounced, prickly and volatile as it was;
it ached to be held, to be pierced
            and parsed—
to be understood was its cry.
By storm it came—
a lullaby sung to the fast-asleep,
as a bridge hovering over fog.
I held out my sword; a squire was I just
recently knighted,
                nascently heroic.

2

She came.
In dance she came,
as the Bolshoi before opening night, unofficial
and rough,
tooling mishap unto mishap and final comfort,
culling given misconceptions into form,
taking from the higher atmosphere, and investing
            the lower air—
O, my defense faltered, shook, wrestled
      (I was charged with anxiety),
confronted, salted,

and as allowing as this was, a fear caught me,
and the base of its force, aligned to its own
                        instructive will,
                        reached into my heart,
and I gave—
but not before I had found ...
before I had been   found!

—ACTING

A center,
culled, straddled,
calibrated,
undermined,
its remnants lurking—

in memories abandoned,
ex-communicated,

outcast,
its potential yearning,
its song lasting longer—

Other sides press
(pretentiously press)
but falsify—
an enemy!

No middle
to its formal riddle.

—AMBULATING CHANGE

The change began,
wobbled to and fro like the rumble
of a dragon's body,
loose—

It set its mark,
hobbled
like the old on a stick
but pulled close,
tugged hard,
ambulated quickly,

life's marrow short-circuiting,
and tangling
with cacophonous irony.

[AMONGST CREATURES SOLD]

Thoughtless matter wails,

and my head upon a crumbling Eden rests:

      "The stuff with which life is covered—
this winged abandonment, flightless, too-bluntly placed
before us,
spills into gutters, short on breath.
I reek from its substance and trail in its valley lost."

AN ENCROACHMENT

It is what comes to the fore
when the time is ripe. It narrows the door
and usurps in power what was once
                filled, and the floor,
bruised as it is by the harshness of dew, nods
like the hesitant flower.
Cry, says the wind, to the distances cry and raze from
the air
the wish to be free; resound like the sun's shine
over and above mother earth. Sigh. Sigh
as the sparrow sighs when its wings deceive—
From the spill of dry wine flee ... fly.
What is a home but a simple encroachment
upon time—
upon time that will end, too soon disagree.

—AN UNTOLD STORY

It does not come from the reaches of a grassy knoll,

for the details form simply—no thundering roll.

The frame itself and its outer spill crashes warmly onto
the scene;

no border falls or rises to abruptly intervene.

This does not come from a non-eventfully founded source
                         (though some may call it worse)!

An untold story tells us nothing, only simmers, and holds
in time,
                until someone's wanted hope glimmers.

It then tumbles gently onto the other's ear

(this happens once in every twenty-seventh year).

ON THE BLINK

Faces are on the blink,
however mute and hidden they may be;
they nurture a decline.
In the whiff of an errant air and a dampness
to their wild façade, there hides
    the truth;

"… and the city falls behind the curtains howling like
a hill
        caving through the sand."

—PICTURING THE PAST

The past
plotted onto a glass container
like a label on a face,
which says,
      "To be filled at once—"
Here, I stop

(for the memory plays
on the hint of a wish to be living
like an innocent
to some truth known,
the lasting tenure of being taper-
ing forward…

cautiously,
a benevolent sea
onto this present's
      occluded form).

RESTRUCTURING—

1.

What shall we do with these fences,
for in their fall
all kinds of demolitions give;
no answer shall infer
on the translation of these times
as when we see them downed in nature,
by sound blurted,
cast upon ground like an icy snow too long ungrateful—
fences sharpened so
tell a story too short to long unfold!
Must we stand them up again?
      (And still, yet again?)

Their circuitous journey impales the matter
further than one would like;
their normal form becomes their fallen shadow, deeply cast.
Only the rains, when the sun has faulted
and danced non-authoritatively
amid a summer's dying trance, can say in all modesty
and strict complacency a border there exists,

but even then, in some heavy pelt,
in lines obscured, fevered whim burns.

We could try to stand these things up, with patience try
and see to what heights those feelings rise
          ginger now, wet—

Un-coated in resolve;
easier said than churlishly done.

Shall we wait and see what comes of it—
see the breadth in the fall,
dance about it, as if for some form newly found?
We might perjure something here or there,
but then, just stepping out the door
incurs some break from time,
        and do these fallen further fall?

2.

They once stood well, crept their edges gratefully,
and even when the modern winds pretended
to be full in fervor,
halting only long enough to be known,
they stood their mettle.

Ah, but ... could something come of it?

What if some turning word arose and tossed
into the mix something of its own intransigence;
Should we rethink this ....
or more, as if in a fit, revive some past no longer viable?
What will have been their cherished manner then
when in non-despairing circumstances
all became
                ... well?

Will these have waned, unseeing,

in their own comfort waxing far from healing?

Could they have foreseen the brim's disaster coming,

would they have added matter to their skin—

written up a new defense?

(We stop and wait for nothing,
trace the matter to its roots as if the answer there were found,
for "I know which heaven steps its step
and holds to quietude
just to show the kin-like frames,
which harbor through the night and un-power every sight
in sightless attitude!")

3.

But if nothing comes nothing comes,

and so be it;

I've stood the standard's banner long enough in such
dear times—

held my own in darkness more than once.

(Surely, sticks abreast lost to wealth may bar no holds divine
if such divineness ne'er be found.)

And friends say, "Let's end it all, give up on it,

stir the cocky pot too full away, toward the winds away.

What care we for muddled wood so nailed as to be untrue,
so quick

as to never again see?

Throw the die, and ride the cup of fond effulgence,

crest upon their doom a final tale

and sing the jig once sung in olden times when where a route became the rule the rule became the route."

Such is the trouble with friends whose such ease
never ends—
who soon embrace obliteration's face and fuel sweet
karma's winds.

how fare ye mates?
Have ye a bare bodkin to share?
—If all is lost,
it's still an easy wear!

4.

Here stand I before this towering fall—

like Ulysses much before his stern return onto a house

no longer his and brimmed with foreign tunes

and pot-bellied games.

[He who sees as only a blind man sees sees heavily and far—

　　　too far to be near.]

(The hammer has been known to fly
far beyond the madman's cold abatement,
too often, its pound a screech
and its heat too hot to stow in fond remembrance;
soon, when the wood is dry
and soon, when the body pastes its scratchy form
onto trees downed, the fields lay ready,
　　　in frothy need—
Nails then are a simple affair;
they march without a care to their point
and enter close to within their knock
onto a man's restraining palm as if through water
with bubbly red matter piercing up.
They ask no questions and form but one answer:
We hold the way

and stabilize a future
so that when the end arrives the hurt
in all its suffering splendor
may decide for ease and forever curb an instance
of swift sound breath on fitfully scattered air.)

The hammer is always the "perhaps",

the nail the "maybe" the hammer slaps.

5.

When all is said and done,
the downed wood has lost its sun.

And yet, let's toy the tune,
and aim for heaven's brighter June.

If no more,
what may we infer from this fine store?

That they may rise?
Some may prove so otherwise.
That they should rise—
as same, more forcefully? In what disguise?
As firm defense?
Under the call of what lens?
To uphold law;
To keep the rawer far from raw?
Yes, and more you say,
to keep the unwanted firm at bay.

I say the fall was given—

to keep fools, humble, who wax too driven!

So, the fall was good;

no, says the owner, as well he should.

But he welcomes compromise,

nail to wood;

Such good is rarely seen round—

never, worldly found!

SMILE FOR ME

Smile for me
the way you do; entangle me
in your arms, for I'm won
and cannot but conform to your embrace.

Smile for me
in your own inimitable way,
and if you alter form,
    keep to your beneficent pace.

Smile for me,
and never let me see the stop
that marshals firm desire
    even to my leaving days.

STAMPED AND LETTERED

Constancy is a wonderful idea,
but it is only an arbiter for a will fitted round
a hole that follows ground too deeply—
in its depths you hear no sound.
What prospers? This same, amid darkness;
into this effort falls the veil of intuitive quickness
by our maker made.
One may call this a weakness.
But to be right with one's self is to be right
with one's freedom: To be by chains unfettered
and still be chained is difficult—
yet only then are we stamped and lettered.

What is the secret to the undying panoply
    of unsorted assistance, which rants
in the corrosive behavior undermining our surge for lucidity?
Is it a new-found virginal birth or "pried-into" advent?
    Is it a cry for help, a remnant
        of a future, still untapped?
        The hold in the eye
renders a rustic flavor to the lie—
The rule of thumb no longer titillates in umbrella effect
            (the luck of the die?)
and the quiet prolongation of the other in the elect
    establishes itself as sect,
      browning in neutrality, this ... our why.

THE FIRE WAS BURNING...

The fire was burning
on the day before that winter's woe—
dated are those inner sounds,
valued back then.
I assumed the breeze would soften, saving openness
like some door slightly ajar.
But judgement decomposes radiantly
in its stand to be jaggedly known and owned;
the hour's borders have gone,
the infernal affliction's tomb usurps,
fetched up
like some sonic boom.
Values are not intoned, and apertures close evenings.
(This barbed entrance fans out, sweet embargo—
a scene from a bard's dying song.)

THE WORK YOU ARE

There is nothing clearer

than the natural smile from a friend dearest

to you; it's in the understanding felt

that opens flower-like mornings. The freshest
sounds come

from such a tie, ever radiant of gesture

    for the work you are—

—THE WAVES SHUFFLE WIDE

The waves shuffle wide

making paths for wishes to travel on;

waiting on the nurture of dream,

I resolve to disagree.

Consider what might otherwise be whim

this side of love,

for most evenings are ridden,

and phases become sea—

The waiting time for wishes is gone.

As for my dreams?

Tomes with holes in them.

—THE MURMURING

The murmuring
of the evening commences
on the plain,
past the sunshine's heat;
a murmuring rain,
a murmuring rain—
and the chirp, chirp
dance
descends
beyond the solitude
as darkness
dangles in the wings;
on the platitude,
on the murmuring,
on the dancing:
juggernaut semblance,
back to life again
as glance,
and more glance!

—THE PUMMELED ROCK

The waves
are happenstance
to its easy flow—
its body's face pummeled
by their briskness,
claws
draining fuel,
collectively impressing
metal upon metal,
hitting,
and the wind
streaming,
  darting.

I stand,
a rock above the shore,
thought drained
from this constant travel,
drained,
from the press
of thunder
and its pummel;

I resist
the undertow,
and yet, trace nothing
but the will
to be tossed

into this abyss, whole
and complete.

Rock against stone,
against metal
as sun begins its daily run,
beautifying
the fog and the cool
caught
in its wings.

I contemplate the darkness of the seal,
the eye indulging in this crawl of death—a
tanker passes.

Its line is empty.

THE SONG

What was that sound which once we heard?
It sounded like a bird.
But was he flirting with the wind,
or simply hurting in his word?
I thought it sounded sparingly like a rhyme from youth—
the kind that muffles in its use.
Not so, for on the bannister it bounced
and clearly entered echo rightly unannounced;
if I too ventured up such meat,
I'd see myself soon hurled onto the master's seat!

Did we not concur when with the breeze the limelight gave?
Did not the ground beneath us lightly slave?

O, such incursions have never bound these rafters,
nor have the poets sung in such hereafters.

My wish is that I'd heard some more
even onto these times just to even up the score,

but all is lost as days begin,
for we'll not see his like again!

Yet, hear me out: His sounds filled our heart's walls too well
to let our minds beneath us dwell;
let memory's lung now flourish without thirst,
so that we may at last be first—
When we envisioned in our modesty his song

did we not rave to heaven all along?
Forthrightly ensconced let our small minds stay; let us be,
as when in youth such eyes so saintly see
a oneness from the world, simply sought and held,
turning forward in the light of constancy.

THE VIRGIN'S SONG

1.

"Drink,
and be renewed,"
she said,
"in love
and matter brewed;

Drink,
and be the part
that slows all time,"
she said,
"for it belongs
to rhyme so rude.

Drink,
and sigh no more,"
she said,
"for love endures
and to its shore
      lays nude."

2.

The vault closed
above my head, and I
became its bed;
by dusk
I shortened,
stood my ground
as dead.
And,
as I rose,
I felt
a ping
which
modulated
high,
but
sound—
and I
was
codified
before
that
jingle's
jeweled
round.

THOMAS

1.

He shuffled,
a vagabond to the remnants of man—
too flushed with wild sound to be heard midst the cries,
and I can't say the air wasn't damp for it wasn't,
and yet,
the cold nurtured hymn,
like a spell from a card game long-ago lost,
all the while bearing down tenderly
(as if it wanted to be lost again); it continued its hum.
He shooed spies of light from his eyes, dangled
        in the crevices of the gutter's charm.

He was a drifter listening to the blare,
an off-the-wall quell wishing the clusters might find their end,

and he shuttered listlessly, a fist of doldrums cast off
only long enough to catch a few winks.

Standing, he tied his string round his pants,
seaman-Sam dungarees dangling from a pile of
rag-tag technicalities,
a miss, muted in her hung-honed face, motioning
        towards him—

And the coat he harbored willed to stray farther from
his body;
it searched for the nearest sea
(he well remembered what the nearest sea looked like—

the younger sea, then filled with quest,
longing to be freer than the God-given nature it'd been given;
it had known then which way the wind tended,
had known then the needless symmetry never found—
only touch, and the breeze on a motionless day, answered,
                    a stern sea then).

2.

Where was he going this day—
today when the skies refused him solace,
when the darkness of the morning willed to never light?
There was this barren brightness coming
from the ticket counter,
and a stone-faced kibitzer rallied in smile.
He merely passed as a rat might;
he merely acted.
            He merely willed to be somewhere.

But not today, not today,
as if on any day!

And people entered the maze, walking
as if the abnormal debated—
as if the way (to wherever) was given formally,
without question.

The lady with the feathered hood—
feather languishing curiously from the side of her cheek—
would soon be given up!
The man with her had to be there;
he pretended more importance
                    than the lady he assisted.

Both boarded,
both escaped from view
quickly,
as they had entered.

3.

A cackle of young ladies
fretting about their goods, as if they had forgotten
where they came from, where they'd been,
wondered through the area—
        Thomas wasn't even there!
They stood close enough to be warranted,
to being with him
as if he were attendant upon them. He moved some;
they moved even more, disappearing
into the good dawn—
quick-flying geese off to their categorized journey.

Others formed lines;
still others filled their proximity with baggage
(and still more baggage). All stopped!
He danced,
like a sailor on leave far from the sirens below
where the flaking masts too far lean—
        He danced.

He then sat, words to his mouth,
like a sandwich long-since cuddled and ruled
a nutritionist's dream
            tabled.

It seemed days—
days when his hands had weathered as half-covered labels—
days upon days of cold hungry nights,
        and nights never won.

He entered his plea,
        and delved—

4.

Like a razor to Mr. Ockham's chin:

This was the simplest solution.
He'd found it.

—The morning issued forth,
like a dagger into the side of a dumb and dodder-
ing oak,
like a simpleton in a corner whimpering

his last.
He could've envisioned a better time,

but no...

For the times drift,
and destiny is a child's gift.

The toss and acceptance of this
chances the kiss—

It is better to live in fear
than to know that the churned-up liquid is near.

TO BE FILTERED SO WELL

When is the written word useless and best kept hidden?
When is it best walled?
When is the readiness to be wordless most likely to bear
witness to the crowning glory
             not yet found and much less called?
When is it time to see this uselessness form out of exis-
tence, drop
into the mayhem of its own undoing and trail like a star in the
western sky—
that which causes no uproar?

It is easy to live in times like these, to be filled with this
unneeded extra strength;
for all will listen for a moment and then segue into the dark
of their minds—
             so happy are we, the unfiltered!

TOO SOON

It may have lasted longer,
and in the longer run advanced beyond its frame;
we may have learned from what faltered,
had it not been wrapped in same—
Reasons abound and wishes filter through the maze like a fog
in the noon-day sun; however, fooled,
we've read the cards and found that death runs hot,
                    hardly ever cooled.
A story is told of one who loved, but nurtured in it too well
—and yet (again) it might be too soon to tell.

ALBERTSON'S
DILEMMA

1.

It hasn't been so long ago when Albertson saw
the wind blow and wallow like the strict brigade on a
terror drive
down the brisk red Rhine.
I knew him when young and full of verve, unbound
and certain that he knew whose arms rose full and whose
cannons curved
the straightest.
Here was a man beset by mission—
a man derived from the gods, Odin over Black Forest,
Valkyrie breasted to the west of France
and beyond.

                 I knew him then and I've known him now.

Still, yet he comes upon a storm few have seen,
and fewer still have claimed as aimed for them, for all as if ...
as if it were God-given.

He saw these winds linger at his side—
saw them caravan beyond their borders much too long
and much too fierce for his strong form to take;
hunkered down as if bolted to the trailer floor, he felt the roar,
and hammering stole his limbs metered onto wave
of flouting flaunting bang!

This tumor trounced those veins of corrugated cardboard
and made them dance about, a ballet out of joint,
a waltz too hazy to be labeled quartered.

No machines here, as the heavens seemed to have set an end
to the dues now tolerated—

2.

Payment on demand was the falsified notion,
and in a nutshell, the only commiseration found.
Ricochets crooned, voices riled the air with off-the-wall tables
and chairs
onto walls no longer there; safety soon became much truer
than the truth had become safe.

Albertson's frame had said, enough!

He would no longer play the target—
no Maginot Line to be tapered to, no stand to correct
and delineate, no reference fighter tank to list, or amble forth
as if parleying for position.

This time...

This time the sight was in view

in a much clearer frame of mind.

Here was the crux of the trembling vigor tumbling all
around him,
heading right once, then left again,
to the skies seconds later, and on towards his own ground.

He ran.
Like a fool too fast to feel, he ran and ran and ran,
into the sticks and flaying branches ran...

Onto the muddied walks of his hinterland he ran and fell.

He seemed to dodge this wherewithal ...

3.

only to find this new hole too low and unforgiving;
the ground began to fill with liquid—a simplicity.
Water filled from the floor much as when he had floundered
in the depths of the Rhine, there too
                              in flight for life.

(Up came the river, and down swam the will;
escape had been of paramount importance then, as now,
but seemingly worse now,
as age creeps in this petty pace too well,
and candles few are ever found.)

"Vaist high, and under done, to the vaist;
                 I vasn't a goner, no."

There was no understanding to be concerned with here
for the matter had been resolved and …

and he would have given his left eye to be hungering in the
war as to be
filled with this much older storm few have categorized
more colorfully than my dear friend Albertson.

—TRIPPED IN GIN

There's nothing to be said
that can weather the ease of a summer bed,
nor is there anything to comply
with the urge in the timing of a bullet's head—
When the rules recede into the abyss
and falter like the farmer's steadfast knees,
so will the matter be much more cynically red!
I would enhance my chances best
by throwing squares onto a slenderly carved hole
ever pronouncing my sentence aloud,
almost always questioning the soul—
but the winds refuse to please
knowing how to unknow the unknown with ease
and still be found clear as summer coal!

Come to me, my darling…
Come to me and rest by the burgeoning dell,
on the banks by the river which dances
like the sounds of the depths churning deep in the well.
Never mind the honey that swelters with bees,
and close your mind to those rivers running to seas—
It's fine to be tripped in gin in the depths of hell!

UNKNOWING

Unknowing—
staggering, melting into the pot
like a butter long after it's been recognized
and seared into matter,
like the tossing wrangle of a beast onto mother earth,
you favor its blanching eye, cake in its warmth,
trounce through its air haltingly,
to the sides seeing, yet not—
It gets hotter the more one enters
        its summer.

VOICELESS SOUND

What is that strength
which wallows in this heart of yours,
that satchels in instance
and then runs away? Is it a commonplace thing,
trudging through an empty mind
like a diamond without a ring, or a finger,
faultlessly dancing in air
readying for the thought to arrive—
the thought which meets the act on its own terms
and then settles for what comes?
Would that I had the wherewithal to twist
your mind around
and set your body down on firmer ground.
Would I not then hear your voice
        as voiceless sound?

WALL TO WALL

Wall to wall and no-bars free tolls the fly
beneath the tree:
                    "I'll find my way. I'll trip their fine alarm.
Next I'll make the leap across
their red settee and cast a bounce upon their song; no ounce
of power grates
my need to satiate,
but now I see a shadow pulsing
like a rough enclosure piecemeal bursting—
It's right upon me now like a soft-lipped slat about to bow.
Must be the softer clap of an Austin City slap:
my time to dance the early morning's sweet romance
                    in easy rhyme."

The music stops, and the splatter's scatter tosses
        as it hops.

—WATER DROPS

The water drops

slowly at first, then quickly

as if it were on the run,

doggedly racing to catch its turn

at a car's wheels

before it too speeds

into oblivion.

It's not a notion to be found

weak in the knees first,

then to be lost entirely to the fact

that love may be

hidden initially—

Notions end.

We settle and catch,

settle,

and catch our understanding

breath.

—WELL-MINDED RUINS

1.

The vents pull through
amid the wind's countermovement;
towards a lower sky claws the shaded shingle.
Its science matters little now,
and hollow falls the mist which nurtures
every heart within.
The evening birds' wings rust to see a limb lip-peeled
and over-run, befriended by the dusty sprinkle
of the devil's tearful cries.
No oasis here to stop the vested travel of a
coated hand—
and all the pews are in a downtown chapel!
The faults which land on the oppressed ground give,
and the returning figure lies complete.
Revolve and agitate, my friends, for disasters
are of the mind.

2.

We breathe as alternates
and the ulterior middle contracts and binds;
a lower composition lower sinks, far from war—
a somber note in some fool's pocket.
An imported sense will not avail itself to this hour,
nor will the alluvial ground weave its hand.
A barren front descends, and every heart must deign

to tote whatever weight intrudes.
Pages refuse to turn and their bird-like punctua-
tion points
to an umbral sunset late in the making;
we are truly members of a tight-lipped family
reddened by a pulverized grit.
To be detained so, as most things are,
and to be voyaging conceitedly, revisits a venue
overly-crossed amid centuries.
Into this are our hopes banked; on this stand
our capitols.
Heaven's answers are of a prime nature,
and its attendant suffering regresses to completion—
yes, my friends, gyrate and disturb for our ruin
                    lies well-minded.

WHAT A VOICE!

What a voice...
It lingered in the sky like a roughly cut gem—
honorifically hailed by saints and good alike, by simpletons
and kings, like-divas and common folk the world over;
tones opened onto clouds erupting, meteors
                    piercing an overcast hue
and in an instant throttling the masses out of their hope-
less reveries
into the thought their words could matter, however off,
or mundane, or not quite ready they may be.
The world waited but found this Quebec curling, hesitating
like the river that starts small; she ended greatly.
O, to have been there with arms folded,
to have been as exiled and to a point all-encompassing
in her goodly-parted brow!

WHAT OLD AGE CANNOT DO:
[AND OTHER PROBLEMS]

It cannot open a can.

It cannot see ahead and thereby transition easily.

It cannot trim well, cut well.

It cannot think exceptionally—
    although, it feels alive, sort of.

It cannot register feelings in a vacuum.

Electricity might be a problem.

It has difficulty editing words.

The new is truly the enemy of the old.

It finds it difficult to hate.

Sympathy is too-well endowed.

The will to will slowly diminishes.

Forgetting the forgotten proves problematical.

Human beings may be falsified.

It is at the mercy of human beings.

Being human finds equality in simply being there.

It hopes it is living in Japan.

WHAT'S BEST

If the voice
is hampered
by the actual roll
of the word,
and the pace
of reason
surges faster
than the mind's capacity
to claim this act,
then,
the odds
are simpler placed

in this longing for the different
and absurd—

(It might be best to skip the notion which seeks to coat
that which has never
been erased.)

WHOM WOULD YOU BE?

Who are you that I may tame you?
Or better yet, whom are you not that I may claim
all that hangs from that frown beneath?
I would rather be lost
in a dungeon, far from the framework of a house too empty to
be real,
pierced by the darkness in my soul,
than see you as you truly are.
If you smile, you do so tenderly as if you were readying juices
deep within that savory seal of salt-sought approval—
And then, on a turn, your frame takes on an anxious flavor;
it pounces on the rudiments of an ancient remedy scat-
tered finely
onto the tip of existence.
Whom might you be, and/or whom would you will to be;
this is the question.
(There is a reminiscence there somewhere.)

YES, FATHER...

The sun rises in the mornings,
and I can sense you're there; you're asking me
about the deeper chasms founded upon the likelihood
that nature might make a turn-around;
I answer with a quip, and say that these mornings might still
be seen
tomorrow, if we listen closely enough, and with deep heart.
You ask about the briskness in the air, and how, when it's so
crisp out, voices
can't be heard, to which I reply, a bit tacitly and dry:
O, voices aren't meant to be overheard too much; and yet,
still others,
so it's said, think voices are loudest when quiet.
Yes, father dear, much has been said about the quietness
of time,
and the blistering silence which comes of it—
so too of the noise in the noiseless, and the vociferousness in
the still and inaudible.
But few words have been said on the littleness of the lowly
deathbed, and how,
when the soft purring hum of a being's last gasp solidifies,
how when in the discreetness of an avalanching solitude
whispers cry,
we stand soundless and unobtrusive.
(It is then that peace sits rather tranquil and uninterrupted in
view of the journey
to come.)

A SINGULARLY STATED WORD

You are
a singularly stated word,
standing firm
and true—
eyes penetrating the chosen emotion:

Love is heart

into which the past falls,

salvation,

the you as part of me,

forever so.

—ALL YOU HAD TO GIVE

You rounded my way,

placed your hands up to my face,

washed the grime back—

I paused

to see this love.

I beckoned, "stay!"

and eternally climbed. In a moment

you were gone.

I heard your voice say:

"Let the matter ride" ...

—ANAESTHETIZED HOPE

The look was right
but wrong
and what might have driven it
sparsely seen
(it would again arise
and string along,
but hardly on a day this lean).
There was no quick reply
to this turn of events;
this was new—
it brought an iffy sigh
to think that this
was you.
I continued work
on the day's quota,
but too much like dead smoke
awkwardly cuddling ground,
in awe,
like anaesthetized hope.

BEING THE VOW

I want the surety of what we had
to rise as then before the sun's fine close,
and chime in sounds of undisclosed beginnings,
to hover over love as then—
let the plains and ever-changing distances sing!
Yet, let us now, out of time and out of want, compel
much less,
like the hand that moves in open space;
let us now transfer beyond this cutting heartless realm
onto the edge of full-fledged breath
and be the vow that wedded beings cling to
when they caress in love.

GOING STEADY

What?
Mistaken hue?
Have my feet fallen
from their step?
Is my head too giddy?
I must admit
there are times I flit
like folly too-well done—
Yet, missteps happen;
it's simpler
to just take a stride,
find its ocean,
fill its gap,
always with an understanding truth.
It's silly
to be thinking time is helpful,
ready—
In olden days,
they called it
going
steady.

HEARTS

I can barely see
your face
amid the debris; your eyes
are a blur.
Your soft touch
gives,
but only in memories
now,
too full
to endure.

HOLD THAT THOUGHT!

Hold that thought,
and keep your sights ahead;
think not on the joy confronting you
before you bed.

Hold that thought,
and ride its firm return
until you're sure that lives are lived
as deaths now burn.

Hold that thought—
It might be right that this day dies
so wild with love's denial
and long-lost sighs.

MY POEM

You're no common catch,
nor simple essay on a school girl's sheet,
nor everyday agenda waiting to be turned and pushed
in the noon day's heat—
And though communal efforts pull this view from heart,
conjoint conjunctions trump and fly beyond
       your bright soul's chart.
Still, I'd rather keep you private,
defend your love, and then, by customizing dint
enrich myself through time outpaced
only by the love you've sent.
                    Love-lost and true am I. Too lame
                    but wise—
                    I long for love and you're quite nice.

—IN SUCH AS THIS

Your task is full of love for the one
who never sees, but there's no sense to this—

What happens when time arrives
to seal the deal with wondrous kiss?

If kissing the wind is the thing that bounds your day,
then where on earth is this clear advice

to make you feel you're on the mend—
that love is on the rise?

Kiss a rose, you might get thorny;
kiss the ground you stand on, that which keeps you stood,

but kissing nothing is the price you pay
for a walled-up game that suits no mood!

I'd sooner you kissed me and tested this time no longer—
kissed the kiss that longs to kiss!

Stand the colder times no more (unless,
of course,
                    you find yourself in such as this)!

LOOK AT HER!

Look at her!
Could one be more beautiful?
She beatifies beauty in an instant!
Look at her, look!
It might be that she affronts eternity, and then,
on the stretch of her hand endures the passage—
what my heart doesn't dare permit!
I could hold like Faust and quietly plead remittance lest
I fall full-force
into a much sadder state.
O, to be a much younger Romeo and appear there
in her eyes vivaciously savored; I would redeem myself,
and encounter the heart I pine for.
This is all I have taken, one look, this ardent look,
and mark—
I am done for!

ONLY NOW

The days have gone before us,

like the nurturing sounds which work to save

forever toppling at our feet.

Only now
      do the birds sing.
I know of no other form of laughter than the kind that holds
to the matter boldly, to the nether thing—
this, that seeks to reign within the richer folds
now lost to the riches lovers bring.

ONTO THE CLIFFS...

What am I moved to say
when the light of day is simply ... day?
Or how am I to know what truth is now
the better way?
I see it in your eyes,
this added notion in my search,
these answers set to rise.
Yet still I ask and will to see you warm
in relevancy—to see you there
in modernity's hold on the chase which reels
amid its hidden fantasy.
O, come with me, my love,
into the coastal plain that shadows none
and see the elemental ebb and flow
imbedded in simplicity's sun.
Come, come—
We'll wash away no truthful tears and raise
our teeming glasses high
onto the cliffs of everlasting joy
and never ever sigh!

YOUR LOVE'S NOT THERE

A fraction of love,
this is too less the pull on the evidence;
it is you who say I may be erring
on some side obscured—
I find this answer lingering,
haunted by the beauty of a dancer no longer there.
The times have swelled. I visualize the dawn
                    and stare.
Your love's not there.

The windows don't reflect,
or we would see each other well—
even when the day is rife with sun's solidity
there's no sell.
What you say drifts back,
indemnifies truth.
Scenic balance, interest, and ease of symmetry
                                    are gone. Alas,
our eyes bear no tomorrow in their view without
the present—
Not even God may see us through our day
                    lest we respond.
Let's open them! And not pretend.
It might just be that truth is simpler in the end.

—SET AS THEY ARE

What was once on tap to run its course
now shows benign remorse;
I cannot find the reason fraught with something simpler
to endorse—

Hearts and loneliness
may never lose their bet,
set as they are so far from net.

So too, those pangs of love descending as they do
upon those innocents caught.

Hearts, as loneliness,
may never lose their bet,
set as they are so far from net.

—SOMEONE'S DIRECTION

The child in you plays at summer woe

and then decides to reach a summer glow;

cries consume your time

encouraged by an alibi unknown—

but what's the question for, if not to see

what's never shown?

—THE FALL TO COME

Stern
is the fall to come

(its cellular demise),

as if the heat of the air
were denouncing the what

for the why of disguise,

and hearts hide beneath
swimmers at sea,

far from sun

churning
like propellered trains

until they're done.

SOFT RUNNING WIND

At times I note
with the calmness of a tender shoot that love may exist
in the most troubling times,
like a soft running wind through the woods
tearing at brush
onto a hideaway specially made,
        attached
to the brow of a long-loving journey
not yet lived.

—THE WINTERS HAVE BEEN MILD

The winters have been mild this year—
milder by far than when we met. And it isn't always fated
to be one with life, not like the sun that finally sets.
I might endear myself to you as one who's always been
a centrally fixed dot; forgive me for being warm,
                         not hot.
I wish the evenings would never bow to the question
of why darkness howls,
for it finds me thinking hard on you as the non-lit fish or
moonlit fowl.
I might endure the occasional faux pas
and sink into this coldness wet. The winters have been mild
this year—milder by far
                than when we met.

—THE YOU THAT'S YOU

Steps at times deceive

and bring the wearer timeless leave,

for when the weight descends

and downward lends the heels unbind
and weave.

Could be that winds embark on a day

too damp and dark … or way,

lost in head-over favor, relieves the
wearer's waiver,

therein falling onto back's delay.

When anxiety attacks anew,

there's always someone there to catch the you
that's you.

—THERE AND THEN

There's no favor to be found
in the need to know what inkling might be learned
from a smart perusal of a piece too new
and not yet settled on the mind; it tears the heart to no end
to shed no blood, and even so, bring the thing into being—
Creation's pure enticements follow through
out of casing into view, like the sweet fine smell of easy dew!
It is a morning's lingering frame of mind not to find the air
too rare
and still be bothered by it all.
O, that she would read the whole so well
that even Mephistopheles might break his dogged cell
and dance the jig upon her desk
transforming life into an arabesque!
The salt-sea air would quickly care, stand up to time
and qualify the rhyme—
There and then would she soon see
the shifting sands of sweetened sanctity,
her eyes now turned to me!

THIS WILL

There is a studied will to all we do;
it is in the talk we think is new, in the things said,
or in the way we say them which make them true: Assets
are something
we all own and cherish, being we are humans in
human carriage,
but all is stayed when we renounce our only fire and dance
                the jig of non-willed marriage.
The risk is great in every step we take (harder as we
move awake),
but when the curves are there, and we are sinfully joyful to
the truth within,
there is no risk, and what was out is in.

—DANCING IN YOUR SKIES

It wasn't but a step to an overture heard—

you set your eyes on me.

I sought a premise, a spoken word, and felt your song

this side eternity. But now, when sound falls dark,

absurd the tone, before this day,

before this morning's dew, before the throated lark stand I

and hear your whisper say:

"Hope resounds when darkness sighs;

I nestle close—

          dancing in your skies."

— SUMMER'S WINE

The wedded vibes
of summer's longing cry
in brackets sit,
and journey quietly
in quiet thought,
on rumors sing, stringing
over wishes.

In the meadows,
echoes cool, love-caught;
no stumbling stones unfold.

(And the cold dips
far beneath
the stern melodic whim;
his hold on nature's stringent time
expiring—)

Warmth, revert, revert!
Or so I pine.

And then, at once,
upon an offbeat chord
in harmonizing form
and keynote sigh,

she comes!
reverberating fine

around a pulsing nerve.

Mark the forceful beat,
an edgy sign
        of longing—

timely summer's wine!

WHAT FARES IN LOVE

Which ground's the best?
Which much sounder than the rest?
Is one above the other bolder for its finer quest?
Or should we perceive the latter
              pass the test?
The wet floor deceives—
Its body's grave un-shores, and wave
abounds in jester's weave,
but will the granite's trust ensure?
In unfasted cast endure?
There is no finer product
for one's as good as he who's got it.
What fares in love is fair all round
for those who lust or laud it.

YOU AND ME

…tantalizing rhythms,
chordal gems of vibrant color,
vibrant pitches too singular to record
and note, with melody
trekking softly through the heart—
a breath of air on a Sunday morning
on the heels of a spring rain.
I can hear joy there,
and the bright arpeggiated sprig of laughter
combing through our thoughts.
This beat is a quiet one,
a songbook reaching through the whole
of life…

CPSIA information can be obtained
at www.ICGtesting.com
Printed in the USA
BVHW08*1940140818
524513BV00002B/9/P

9 781525 530869